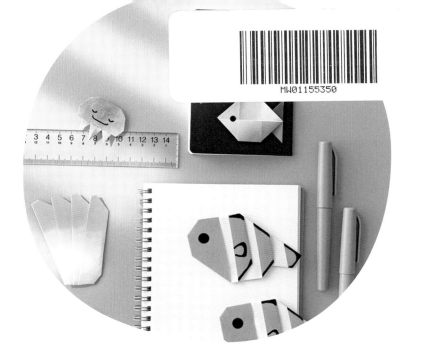

# KAWAII
# Origami Animals

*Fold Adorable Paper Cats, Dogs, Bugs and More!*

Kamikey

**TUTTLE** Publishing

Tokyo | Rutland, Vermont | Singapore

# Contents

## Part 1 | Cute Critters

## Dogs and Cats

### Folding Instructions

## Small Creatures and Birds

### Folding Instructions

## Insects and Plants

### Folding Instructions

## Aquarium

### Folding Instructions

## Zoo

### Folding Instructions

## Small Sea Creatures

### Folding Instructions

## Animal Cosplay

## Folding Instructions

## Part 2 | Small Animal Items

## Pocket Items

### Folding Instructions

## Animal Accessories

### Folding Instructions

Congratulations

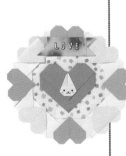

# Projects for Spring

Spring is a season full of celebrations, such as the Doll Festival (Hina Matsuri), graduations, school entrances, and Children's Day. Let's celebrate the growth and new beginnings of children with a wreath adorned with animals.

April

# March

# May

Be
Healthy

金

# Projects for Summer

Even on stormy days during the heat of summer, enjoy decorating with fresh hydrangeas and beach-themed wreaths! Pair them with items like small bottles for a stylish space. It's also lovely to create a Milky Way effect by placing many stars around a Tanabata wreath.

June

# August

# July

# Projects for Autumn

Rabbits making mochi under the moonlit sky, surrounded by colorful trees and living creatures. For Halloween, decorate with wreaths of various sizes. The spooky characters will liven things up!

September

# October

# November

11

# Projects for Winter

A Christmas wreath made from special textured paper looks like something from a storybook. Decorate the New Year's frame with lavish Japanese patterns, or thoughtfully assemble Valentine's Day wreaths with heart patterns and colors.

December

# January

# February

# Folding Diagrams Used in This Book

### Fold Along the Dashed Line

Valley Fold Line

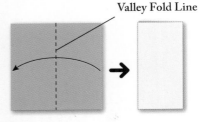

Fold toward yourself along the dashed line.

### Fold Back

Mountain Fold Line

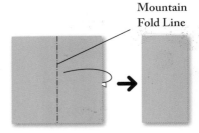

Fold away from yourself along the dashed line.

### Cut with Scissors

Cut along the bold line with scissors.

### Make a Crease

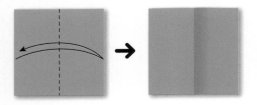

Fold along the dashed line to make a crease, then return to the original position.

### Step Fold

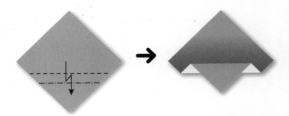

Fold up along the top dashed line, then fold back down again on the bottom folded line.

### Inside Reverse Fold

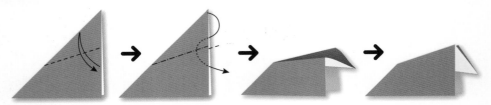

Fold through both layers along the dashed line to make a crease, unfold, and then fold the corner inside.

### Flip Symbol

Flip the origami over.

### Change Direction Symbol

Rotate the origami to change its orientation.

### Open a Pocket Symbol

Open a pocket in the folded origami.

### Zoom In Symbol

Starting with the following diagram, the images will be enlarged.

# Origami Base Folds
## Square Base & Crane Base

In this book, we primarily use standard size origami paper, 6 × 6 in (15 × 15 cm).

**1** Fold in half edge to edge both ways. Unfold.

**2** Fold in half and unfold to make a crease.

**3** Fold backward in half and unfold to make a crease.

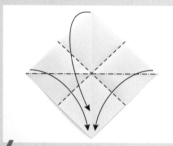

**4** Collapse the paper along the creases.

**5** Step **4** in progress.

**6** The Square Base is completed. For the Crane Base, fold the flaps to the center and unfold.

Square Base

**7** Fold along the dashed line and unfold to make a crease.

**8** Open the pocket and flatten it.

**9** The step **8** pocket is open.

**10** Step **8** is completed. Flip it over.

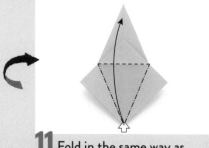

**11** Fold in the same way as steps **6–9**.

**12** The Crane Base is completed.

Crane Base

# Origami Base Folds

## Blintz Base

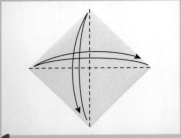

**1** Fold in half corner to corner both ways. Unfold.

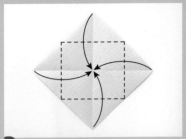

**2** Fold the corners to the center.

**3** The Blintz Base is completed.

## Kite Base

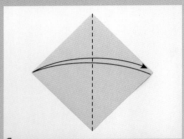

**1** Fold in half corner to corner. Unfold.

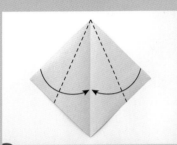

**2** Fold the top edges to the center.

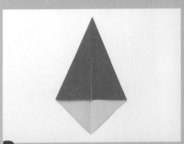

**3** The Kite Base is completed.

## Fish Base

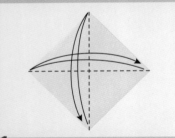

**1** Fold in half corner to corner both ways. Unfold.

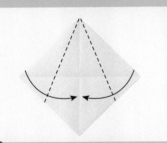

**2** Fold the top edges to the center.

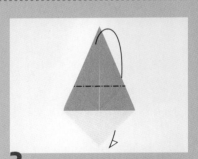

**3** Mountain fold the paper in half behind.

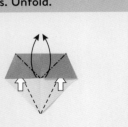

**4** Open the pockets and flatten.

**5** Step 4 in progress.

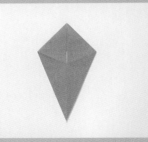

**6** The Fish Base is completed.

# Origami Base Folds
## Waterbomb Base

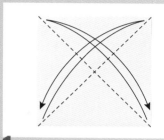

**1** Fold in half corner to corner both ways. Unfold.

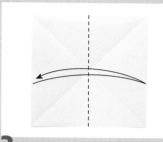

**2** Fold in half edge to edge. Unfold.

**3** Mountain fold the paper in half behind.

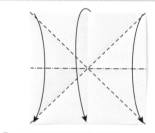

**4** Collapse the paper along the creases.

**5** Step 4 in progress.

**6** The Waterbomb Base is completed.

## Pig Base

**1** Fold in half corner to corner both ways. Unfold.

**2** Fold in half edge to edge. Unfold.

**3** Fold the left and right edges to the center.

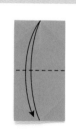

**4** Fold in half top to bottom. Unfold.

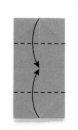

**5** Fold the top and bottom edges to the center.

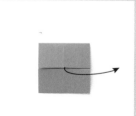

**6** Pull out the inner corner, pivot and flatten.

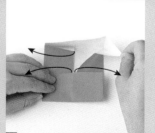

**7** Step 6 in progress. Do the same for the other three corners.

**8** The Pig Base is completed.

# Dogs and Cats

Dogs and cats are the most popular domestic pets. Many people consider them to be part of the family. These are adorable decorations, but they also make great gifts for dog and cat lovers.

**Dogs**

Instructions begin on page 20

## Cats

Instructions begin on page 26

I'm popular worldwide! I'm a friendly, confident Japanese dog.

## Body

Start by folding the paper in half vertically and horizontally.

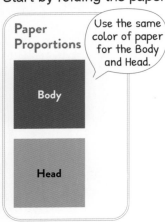

**Paper Proportions**

Use the same color of paper for the Body and Head.

Body

Head

**1**

Fold the top and bottom edges to the center.

**2**

Fold the left and right edges to the center.

**3**

Reversing the folds from here on causes the tail to emerge from the left.

Grasp the inner corner, pivot it down, and flatten it into a triangle.

**4**

Step **3** in progress.

**5**

Fold the corners to meet at the center.

**6**

Fold the flap along the dashed line, and then turn the paper over.

**7**

The Body is completed.

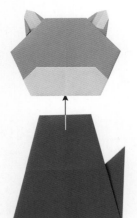

Insert the Body into the pocket of the Head.

Finished!

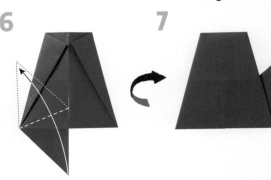

Wishing You Continued Good Health!

Make a smaller version, glue it to a postcard, and use it as a New Year's card!

**Postcard**
Approximately 6 × 4 in (15 × 10 cm)

**Flower - Large (page 117)**
3 × 3 in (7.5 × 7.5 cm)

**Flower - Small**
2 × 2 in (5 × 5 cm)

**Shiba Inu**
Head & Body: 3 × 3 in (7.5 × 7.5 cm)

**Flower - Medium**
2⅓ × 2⅓ in (6 × 6 cm)

# Head

Start by folding it in half vertically to create a crease.

**1**

Fold in half.

**2**

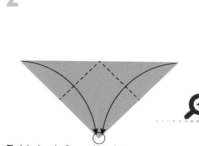

Fold the left and right corners to align with the corner marked ○.

**3**

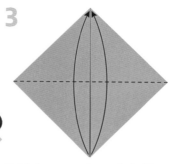

Fold the upper layer in half.

**4**

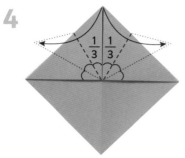

Fold the upper layer as indicated.

**5**

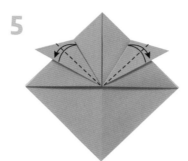

Align the edges of the paper, crease, and unfold.

**6**

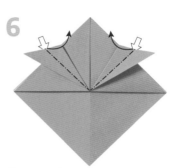

Open pockets at the ✍✍ symbols, and then squash flat.

**7**

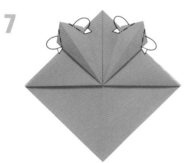

Fold the corners back as indicated, and then turn the paper over.

**8**

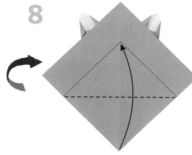

Fold the top layer as indicated.

**9**

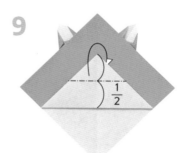

Fold the tip of the flap behind.

**10**

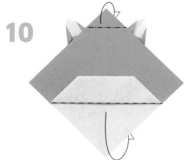

Fold behind at two locations as indicated.

**11**

Fold behind at two locations as indicated.

**12**

The Head is completed. Draw on the face.

## Part 1 — Toy Poodle

Photo on page 18

Photo on page 18

Enhance the dog-like appearance with a plump, rounded muzzle!

## Muzzle

Start by folding the paper in half vertically to create a crease.

### Paper Proportions

The Muzzle is ¼ the size of the Head.

Head and Body

Muzzle

For the Body, see page 20.

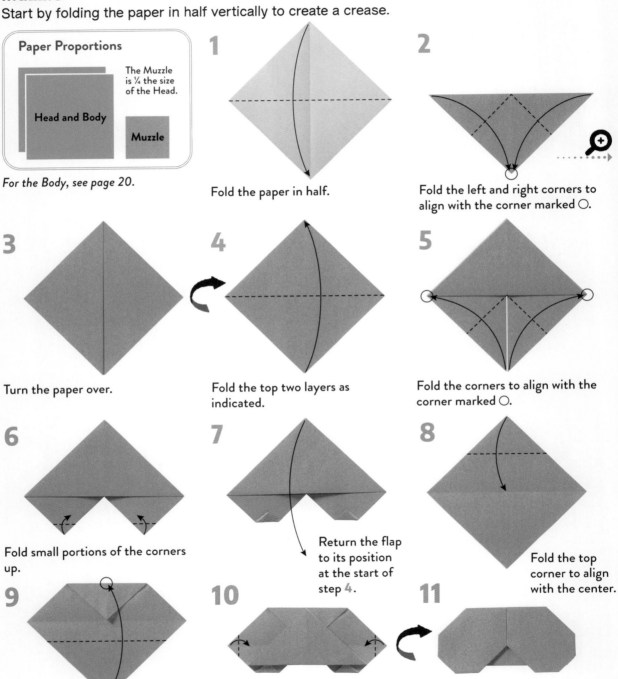

**1** Fold the paper in half.

**2** Fold the left and right corners to align with the corner marked ○.

**3** Turn the paper over.

**4** Fold the top two layers as indicated.

**5** Fold the corners to align with the corner marked ○.

**6** Fold small portions of the corners up.

**7** Return the flap to its position at the start of step 4.

**8** Fold the top corner to align with the center.

**9** Fold the corners of both layers to align with the position marked ○.

**10** Fold small portions of the corners in, and then turn the paper over.

**11** The Muzzle is completed.

# Head

Start by folding step **1** of the Muzzle (see opposite).

**1**

Fold the corners of both layers to align with the position marked ○. Crease and unfold.

**2**

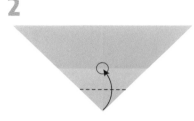

Fold the corners of both layers to align with the position marked ○.

**3**

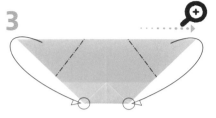

Fold the left and right corners behind to align with the corners marked ○.

**4**

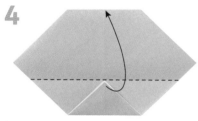

Pull up the flap, align it with the edge of the paper, and then flatten.

**5**

Fold the bottommost corners to align with the positions marked ○.

**6**

Fold small portions of the corners up to meet the edge.

**7**

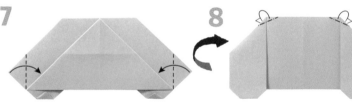

Fold the corners in, and then turn the paper over.

**8**

Blunt the corners by folding small portions back as indicated.

**9**

The Head is completed. Attach the Muzzle and draw on the face.

Finished!

Make the Body of the Shiba Inu (page 20) and attach the Head.

## Size chart for the dog decorations (page 18)

**Toy Poodle (large)**
Head and Body:
6 × 6 in (15 × 15 cm),
Muzzle:
3 × 3 in (7.5 × 7.5 cm)

**Toy Poodle (small)**
Head and Body:
4¾ x 4¾ in (12 x 12 cm),
Muzzle:
2⅓ x 2⅓ in (6 × 6 cm)

**Shiba Inu (page 20)**
Head and Body:
6 × 6 in (15 × 15 cm)

**Chihuahua (page 24)**
Head: 6 × 6 in (15 × 15 cm),
Body: 6 × 3 in (15 x 7.5 cm),
Muzzle: 2 × 2 in (5 × 5 cm)

Big ears are part of the charm!

## Body

Start by folding the paper in half vertically and horizontally to install creases.

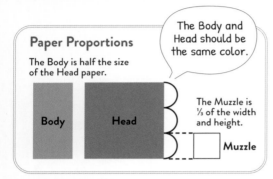

### Paper Proportions

The Body is half the size of the Head paper.

Body | Head

The Body and Head should be the same color.

The Muzzle is ⅓ of the width and height.

Muzzle

*Instructions for the Muzzle: page 22.*

**1**

Fold the bottom edge to the center and unfold.

**2**

Fold the bottom edge to the step **1** crease.

**3**

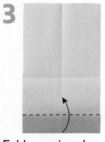

Fold up using the existing crease.

**4**

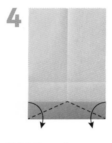

Fold flaps down as indicated.

**5**

Reversing the folds from here on causes the body to face to the right.

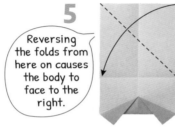

Fold as indicated.

**6**

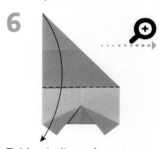

Fold as indicated.

**7**

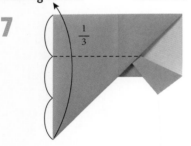

⅓

Fold the flap up as indicated.

**8**

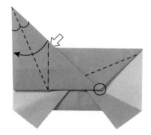

Open a pocket at the ✍ symbol and flatten the triangular part while folding it in half.

**9**

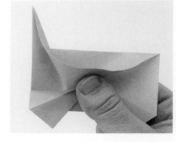

Flatten the part marked ○ in the photo at left.

**10**

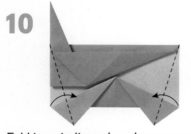

Fold in as indicated, and turn over.

**11**

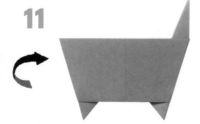

The Body is completed.

# Head

Start by folding the paper in half vertically and horizontally to install creases.

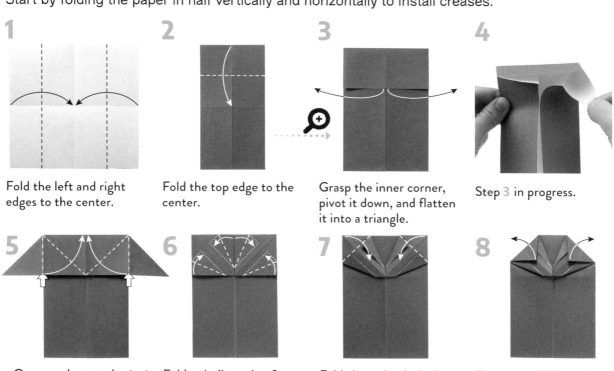

**1**

Fold the left and right edges to the center.

**2**

Fold the top edge to the center.

**3**

Grasp the inner corner, pivot it down, and flatten it into a triangle.

**4**

Step 3 in progress.

**5**

Open pockets at the ✏✏ symbols, then squash flat.

**6**

Fold as indicated at four locations.

**7**

Fold along the dashed lines.

**8**

Return the folds made in steps 6 and 7.

**9**

Open pockets at the ✏✏ symbols, then squash flat.

**10**

Step 9 in progress.

**11**

Align the bottom corners to the center crease and fold.

**12**

Fold to bring the parts marked ○ together.

**13**

Fold three corners behind to round the shape.

**14**

The Head is completed. Create the Muzzle (page 22), attach it, and draw on the face.

Finished!

Attach the Head to the Body.

25

# Cat
Photo on page 19

Try folding cats with various colors and paper patterns!

## Body

Follow steps **1–3** of the Fish Base (page 16), and then rotate to match the orientation below.

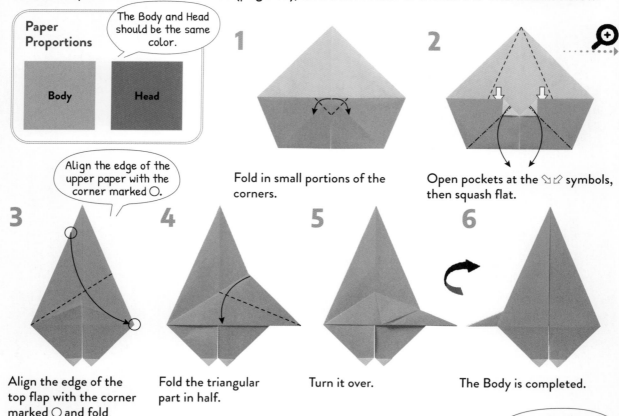

Paper Proportions

The Body and Head should be the same color.

Body

Head

**1** Fold in small portions of the corners.

**2** Open pockets at the ⬒⬓ symbols, then squash flat.

Align the edge of the upper paper with the corner marked ○.

**3** Align the edge of the top flap with the corner marked ○ and fold.

**4** Fold the triangular part in half.

**5** Turn it over.

**6** The Body is completed.

### Crossover ideas!

**Halloween wreath made from models from Kamikey's other books**

**From *Kamikey's Seasonal Origami* (ISBN: 9784537216417):**
Hexagonal Wreath (page 126)
6 × 6 in (15 × 15 cm), 6 pieces

**From *Kamikey's Heartfelt Gift Origami* (ISBN: 9784537219517):**
Witch (page 108)
Body: 6 × 6 in (15 × 15 cm)
Hat: 3 × 3 in (7.5 × 7.5 cm)
Broom Bristles
3 × 3 in (7.5 × 7.5 cm)
Broom Handle
3 × 1½ in (7.5 × 3.75 cm)
Pumpkin (Large, page 106)
4¾ × 4¾ in (12 × 12 cm)

Combine with models from other books for more fun!

Pumpkin (Small)
3 × 3 in (7.5 × 7.5 cm)

Cat (Head & Body)
3 × 3 in (7.5 × 7.5 cm)

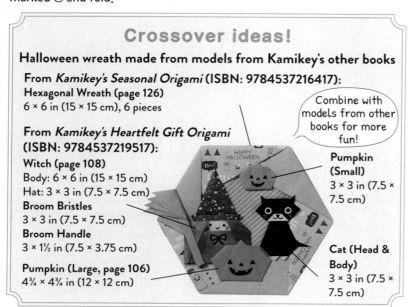

When decorating together with the dog as shown on page 19, make them both with smaller paper, such as ¼ size.

Finished!

Insert the Body into the Head and glue together.

# Head

Start by folding it in half left to right to create a crease. Unfold.

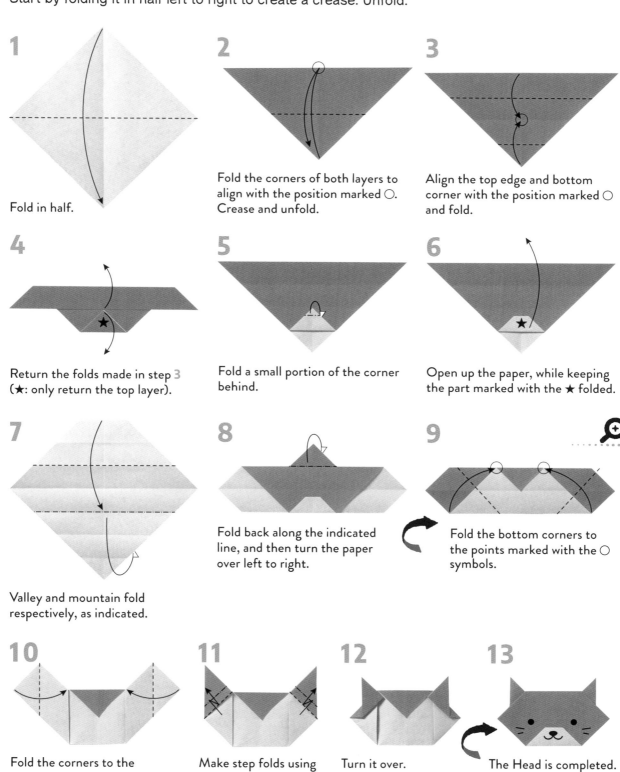

**1**

Fold in half.

**2**

Fold the corners of both layers to align with the position marked ○. Crease and unfold.

**3**

Align the top edge and bottom corner with the position marked ○ and fold.

**4**

Return the folds made in step 3 (★: only return the top layer).

**5**

Fold a small portion of the corner behind.

**6**

Open up the paper, while keeping the part marked with the ★ folded.

**7**

Valley and mountain fold respectively, as indicated.

**8**

Fold back along the indicated line, and then turn the paper over left to right.

**9**

Fold the bottom corners to the points marked with the ○ symbols.

**10**

Fold the corners to the indicated intersections.

**11**

Make step folds using the indicated lines.

**12**

Turn it over.

**13**

The Head is completed. Draw on the face.

# Small Creatures and Birds

Starting with the flying squirrel, we've gathered a collection of adorable creatures. You can even write a message on their bellies to give as a gift!

**Flying Squirrel**

Instructions on page 34

**Hedgehog**

Instructions on page 34

## Budgerigar and Canary

Instructions on page 36

## Hamster

Instructions on page 30

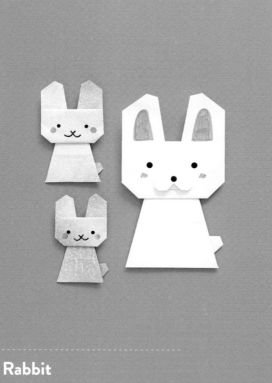

## Rabbit

Instructions on page 32

## Owl

Instructions on page 38

Give it a sunflower seed to hold in its tiny hands

## The Body
Start by folding the paper in half vertically and horizontally to install creases.

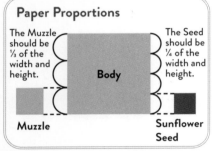

### Paper Proportions

The Muzzle should be ⅓ of the width and height.

**Body**

The Seed should be ¼ of the width and height.

**Muzzle**

**Sunflower Seed**

*Muzzle instructions: page 22*

**1**

Fold the bottom to the center.

**2**

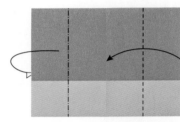

Mountain and valley fold, as indicated.

**3**

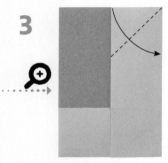

Align the corner with the edge of the paper and fold.

**4**

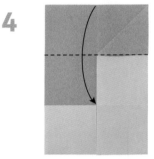

Fold along the dashed line.

**5**

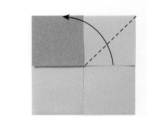

Fold the top layer along the dashed line.

**6**

Open the fold made in step **4** temporarily (**7**), pull out the inner corner and push it upward (**8**).

**7**

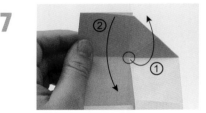

Opened section. Bring the ○ corner upward ①, then return the opened section to its place ②.

**8**

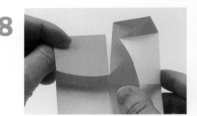

Inner corner is now brought upward.

**9**

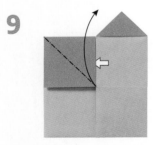

Open the ⇦ pocket and flatten.

**10**

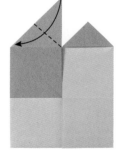

Align the corners and fold.

**11**

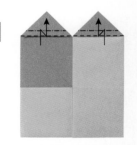

Fold as indicated to step fold.

Continues

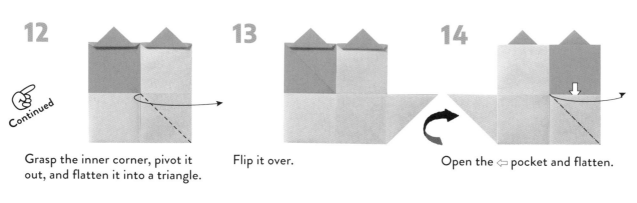

**12** Grasp the inner corner, pivot it out, and flatten it into a triangle.

**13** Flip it over.

**14** Open the ⬅ pocket and flatten.

**15** Fold as indicated.

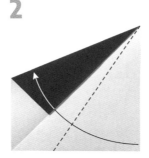

**16** Fold behind as indicated.

**17** Fold behind as indicated.

## Sunflower Seed

Start by folding in half diagonally. Unfold.

**1** Fold the top edge to the diagonal crease.

**2** Align the right edge with the folded edge and fold.

**3** Align the bottom left corner with the top edge of the paper and fold.

Finished!

The Body is completed. Draw on the face and attach the Muzzle (page 22).

**4**

Fold in the corners and flip it over.

Finished!

Draw a pattern.

It's cute when you have the hamster hold it in its paws!

# Rabbit

Photo on page 29

Write a message on the body and attach it to a gift!

## Head

Start by folding the paper in half side to side to install a vertical crease.

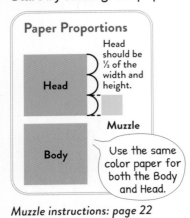

**Paper Proportions**

Head should be ⅓ of the width and height.

Head

Muzzle

Body

Use the same color paper for both the Body and Head.

*Muzzle instructions: page 22*

**1**

Fold in half.

**2**

Fold the top layer along the dashed lines and make creases.

**3**

Fold the top layer along the dashed lines and stand up the point marked with a ★.

**4**

Flatten the middle pocket into a triangle and fold it along the existing crease.

**5**

Fold the corners to meet the circles.

**6**

Fold the bottom corners to meet at the center.

**7**

Fold a small portion of the ear corners down. Fold the bottom corner to the circle. Turn it over.

**8**

The Head is completed. Make and attach the Muzzle (page 22), and draw on the face.

## Body

Start after folding the Body of the Shiba Inu up to step **5** (page 20).

**1**

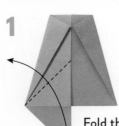

Reversing the folds (starting on page 20) places the tail on left.

Fold the flap along the dashed line.

**2**

Fold the corner to meet the edge of the paper.

**3**

Fold so that the corner sticks out a bit.

**4**

Fold a small portion of the corner. Turn the paper over.

**5**

The Body is completed.

*Finished!*

Attach the Head to the Body.

# Hedgehog

Photo on page 28

I'm a very popular pet! Just looking at me is soothing.

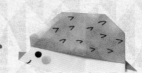

Start by folding the paper in half vertically, horizontally, and diagonally to the right to install creases.

If you start by folding it the other way, it will face to the right.

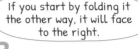

**1**

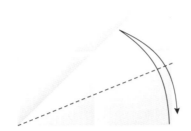

Fold to create a crease bisecting the angle.

**2**

Blunt the tip of corner ①. Fold corner ② to bisect the angle.

**3**

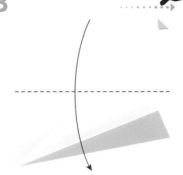

Fold in half.

**4**

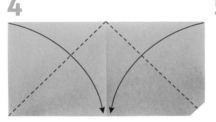

Fold the corners to meet at the center.

**5**

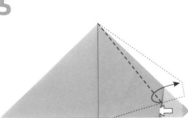

Open a pocket in the upper flap, pivot, and flatten.

**6**

Step 5 in progress.

**7**

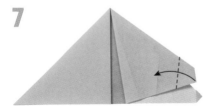

Fold the flap along the dashed line.

**8**

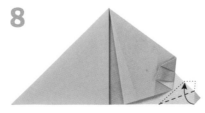

Fold the lower flap as indicated.

**9**

Fold the corner to meet the center.

**10**

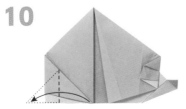

Fold a portion of the corner back so that it sticks out a bit.

**11**

Fold down the top corner to round the form. Turn the paper over.

Finished!

Draw on the face and pattern.

# Flying Squirrel

Photo on page 28

## Head

Start by folding the paper in half vertically and horizontally to install creases.

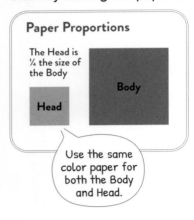

**Paper Proportions**

The Head is ¼ the size of the Body

Head

Body

Use the same color paper for both the Body and Head.

**1**

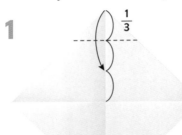

$\frac{1}{3}$

Fold along the dashed line.

**2**

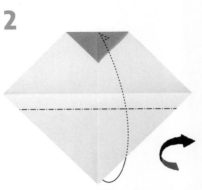

Mountain fold the bottom corner behind to meet the top edge of the paper. Turn the paper over.

**3**

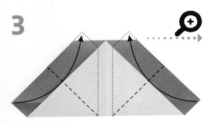

Fold so that the corners stick out a bit.

**4**

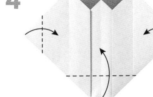

Fold along the dashed lines. Turn the paper over.

**5**

The Head is completed. Draw on the face.

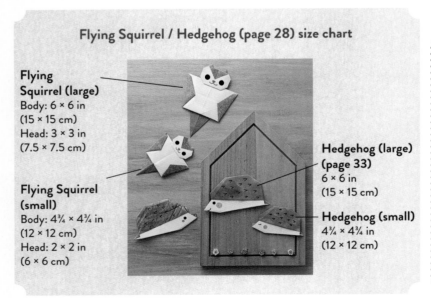

Flying Squirrel / Hedgehog (page 28) size chart

**Flying Squirrel (large)**
Body: 6 × 6 in (15 × 15 cm)
Head: 3 × 3 in (7.5 × 7.5 cm)

**Flying Squirrel (small)**
Body: 4¾ × 4¾ in (12 × 12 cm)
Head: 2 × 2 in (6 × 6 cm)

**Hedgehog (large) (page 33)**
6 × 6 in (15 × 15 cm)

**Hedgehog (small)**
4¾ × 4¾ in (12 × 12 cm)

Finished!

Attach the Head to the Body.

# Body

Start by folding up to step **9** of the Crane Base (page 15).

**1**

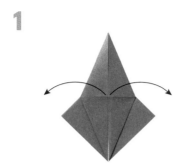

Unfold everything to reveal the white side.

**2**

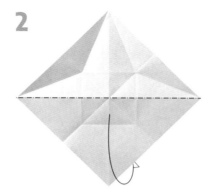

Fold in half to the back.

**3**

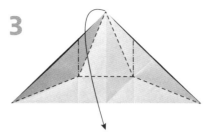

Use the existing creases to collapse the paper.

**4**

Step **3** in progress.

**5**

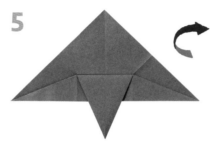

Turn it over.

**6**

Fold the corner to meet the circled point. Crease and unfold.

**7**

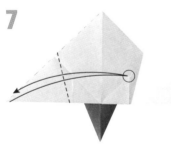

Fold the corner to meet the circled point. Crease and unfold.

**8**

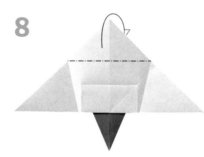

Fold to the back as indicated.

**9**

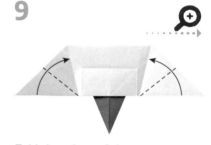

Fold the edges of the paper to meet the creases.

**10**

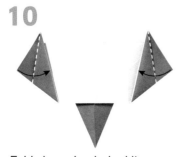

Fold along the dashed lines.

**11**

Fold down the corners.

**12**

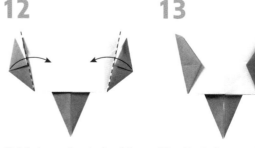

Fold along the dashed lines.

**13**

The Body is completed.

# Budgerigar

Photo on page 29

## Head

Start by folding the paper in half vertically to install a crease.

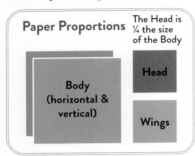

| Paper Proportions | The Head is ¼ the size of the Body |
|---|---|

Body (horizontal & vertical)

Head

Wings

*The Budgerigar and Canary are the same size.*

**1**

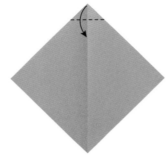

Fold along the dashed line—about ½ in (12 mm) if using 3 in (7.5 cm) square origami paper.

**2**

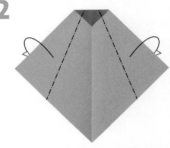

Fold the edges of the paper behind to meet the center crease.

**3**

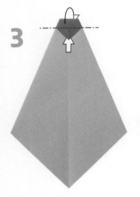

Pick up the corner and pivot the top portion to the back.

**4**

Fold the bottom corner behind as indicated and tuck it inside.

**5**

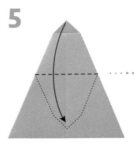

Fold along the dashed line.

**6**

Fold to the back as indicated to round the head.

**7**

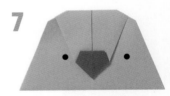

The Head is completed. Draw on the eyes.

## Crossover ideas!

**Compose a Respect-for-the-Aged Day decoration from various sources.**

Combine with origami from other books for more fun!

From *Kamikey's Kawaii Seasonal Origami* (ISBN: 9784537218282)
**Chrysanthemum (page 44)**
6 × 6 in (15 × 15 cm)
**Leaf (page 129)**
2 × 2 in (5 × 5 cm)

**Frame (this book, page 142)**
6 × 6 in (15 × 15 cm), 4 pieces

**Canary**
Body: 6 × 6 in (15 × 15 cm)
Head: 3 × 3 in (7.5 × 7.5 cm)

## Canary

For the Canary, make the folded corner in step **1** slightly larger. The Body and Wings are folded the same as for the Budgerigar.

## Body (horizontal)

Start from the Kite Base (page 16).

**1**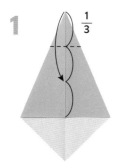

$\frac{1}{3}$

Fold along the dashed line.

**2**

Fold along the dashed line.

**3**

Fold the bottom edge to meet the edge of the step 2 flap.

**4**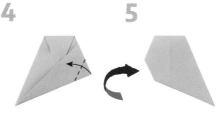

Fold in the corner and turn the paper over.

**5**

The Body (horizontal) is completed.

## Wings

Start by folding up to step **3** of the Sunflower Seed (page 31).

**1**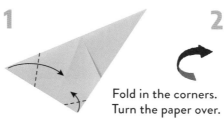

Fold in the corners. Turn the paper over.

**2**

The Wings are completed.

## Body (vertical)

Start after folding step **1** of the Body (horizontal).

**1**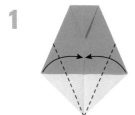

Fold the corners to the center.

**2**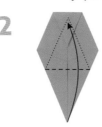

Fold along the dashed line.

**3**

Fold the flap back down diagonally. Turn the paper over.

**4**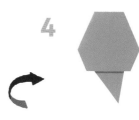

The Body (vertical) is completed.

## Canary

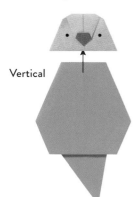

Vertical

Horizontal

Insert the Body into the pocket of the Head and glue it.

Wing

Glue on the Wing.

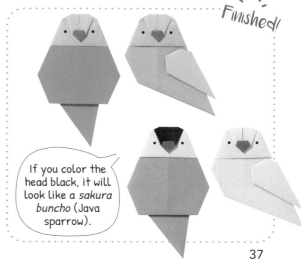

Finished!

If you color the head black, it will look like a *sakura buncho* (Java sparrow).

37

I'm considered a lucky creature, making me a perfect gift!

## Eyes and Beak Parts

Start by folding the paper in half horizontally to install a crease.

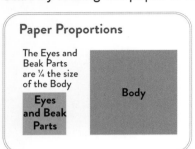

**Paper Proportions**

The Eyes and Beak Parts are ¼ the size of the Body

Eyes and Beak Parts

Body

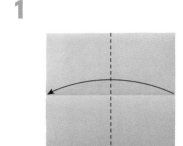

**1**

Fold in half.

**2**

$\frac{1}{3}$

Fold along the dashed line.

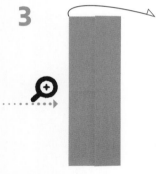

**3**

Swing the bottom layer to the right.

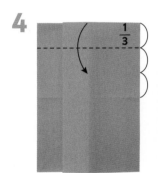

**4**

$\frac{1}{3}$

Fold along the dashed line.

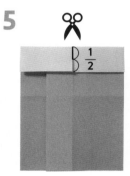

**5**

$\frac{1}{2}$

Cut through all layers along the span indicated by the bold line.

**6**

Fold in the corners.

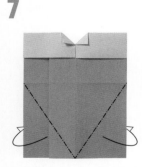

**7**

Fold the corners behind along the dashed lines.

**8**

Fold along the dashed line.

**9**

Fold the corners to the back.

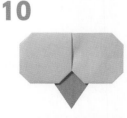

**10**

The Eyes and Beak Parts are completed.

# Body

Start by folding the paper in half vertically and horizontally to install creases.

**1**

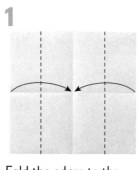

Fold the edges to the center.

**2**

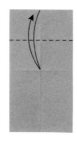

Fold the top edge to the center and unfold.

**3**

Open pockets at the ⇨ ⇦ symbols and flatten.

**4**

Step 3 in progress.

**5**

Fold the corner to the back.

**6**

Fold the flaps up diagonally.

**7**

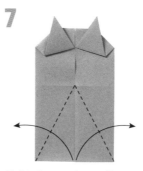

Fold the top layer flaps along the dashed lines.

**8**

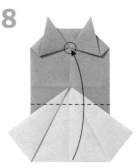

Fold the edge of the paper to meet the circled location.

**9**

Fold the side flaps to the back as indicated. Turn the paper over.

**10**

Fold the corners to the back along the dashed lines.

**11**

The Body is completed.

Tuck the Eyes and Beak Parts under the triangular flap of the Body and glue it in place.

Finished!

Draw on the eyes.

# Insects and Plants

Snails, maple leaves and other insects and plants evoke a sense of the seasons. Skillfully incorporate them into seasonal decorations.

**Rainy Day Decoration**

Instructions on page 45

## Simple Maple

Instructions on page 46

## Dragonfly

Instructions on page 47

## Tree and Bagworm

Instructions on pages 48–49

Turn a single sheet into a large hydrangea flower!

## Flower

Start from the Pig Base (page 17).

**Paper Proportions**

Flower (large)

The Leaf and small Flower are ¼ the size of the large Flower

Flower (small) | Leaf

*The folding methods for the large Flower and small Flower are the same.*

**1**

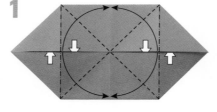

Open pockets at the ⇓⇑ symbols and flatten.

**2**

Turn the paper over.

**3**

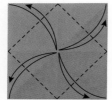

Fold the corners to the center to install creases. Unfold.

**4**

Fold the corners to meet the step **3** creases. Unfold.

**5**

Unfold everything to reveal the colored side.

**6**

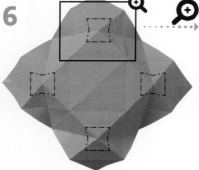

Opened view. Steps **7–10** show detail views.

**7**

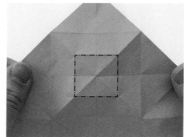

Convert all the creases in the square to mountain creases.

**8**

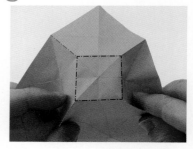

Pinch the red mountain-fold lines at the four corners to make it three-dimensional.

**9**

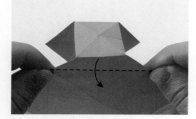

Fold along the dashed line and collapse the form to the inside.

42

**10**

Folding in progress. Fold the other three parts the same way as steps **7–10**.

**11**

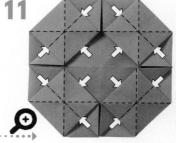

Open pockets where indicated and raise up outward-facing three-dimensional flaps.

Continues

# Leaf

**1**

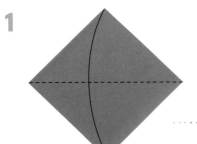

Fold in half.

**2**

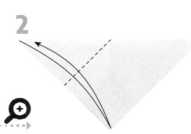

Bring the corners together and install a crease.

**3**

Fold the corners to meet the circled location. Crease and unfold.

**4**

Accordion fold to install creases.

**5**

Fold along the dashed line.

**6**

Open the top layer of paper along the edge of the flap folded in step **5**, and then rotate the paper to change its orientation.

**7**

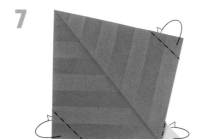

Fold the corners to the back.

**8**

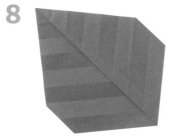

The Leaf is completed.

Finished!

**12**

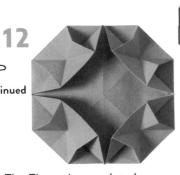

Continued

The Flower is completed.

Create a small Flower with ¼ size paper and place it inside the large Flower to make a deluxe blossom.

43

When paired with the Hydrangea (page 42), they make a perfect decoration for summer!

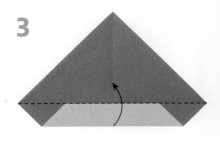

Start by folding the paper in half vertically and horizontally to install creases.

**1**

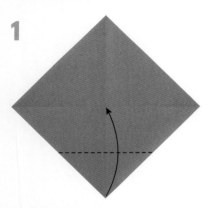

Fold the bottom corner to the center.

**2**

Fold the bottom edge of the paper to meet the horizontal crease.

**3**

Fold along the existing crease.

**4**

If you fold it the other way from here, it will face to the right.

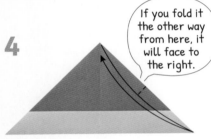

Fold corner to corner to install a pinch mark at the edge.

**5**

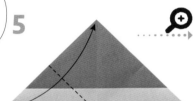

Fold corner to corner.

**6**

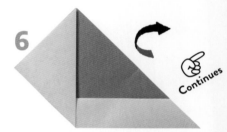

Turn the paper over.

Continues

---

## Crossover ideas!

**Gift bags made using a design from another Kamikey book.**

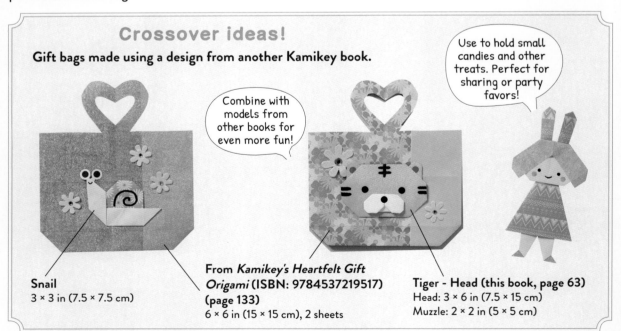

Combine with models from other books for even more fun!

Use to hold small candies and other treats. Perfect for sharing or party favors!

**Snail**
3 × 3 in (7.5 × 7.5 cm)

From *Kamikey's Heartfelt Gift Origami* (ISBN: 9784537219517) (page 133)
6 × 6 in (15 × 15 cm), 2 sheets

**Tiger - Head** (this book, page 63)
Head: 3 × 6 in (7.5 × 15 cm)
Muzzle: 2 × 2 in (5 × 5 cm)

**Continued**

**7**

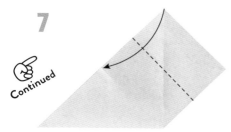

Fold the edge of the paper to meet the crease.

**8**

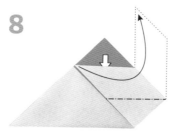

Open a pocket from the ⇩ symbol and flatten.

**9**

Step **8** in progress.

**10**

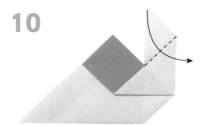

Fold along the dashed line.

**11**

Fold so that the corner sticks out a bit.

**12**

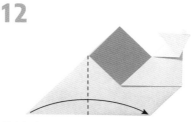

Fold along the dashed line.

**13**

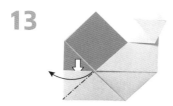

Open a pocket from the ⇩ symbol and flatten.

**14**

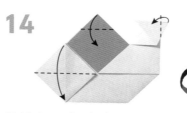

Fold along the dashed lines and turn the paper over.

Finished!

Draw eyes on cut paper circles, or layer and apply large white and small black round stickers to create eyes. Draw the mouth and spiral pattern.

### Rainy Day Decoration (page 40) size chart

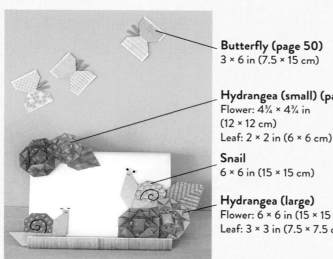

**Butterfly (page 50)**
3 × 6 in (7.5 × 15 cm)

**Hydrangea (small) (page 42)**
Flower: 4¾ × 4¾ in
(12 × 12 cm)
Leaf: 2 × 2 in (6 × 6 cm)

**Snail**
6 × 6 in (15 × 15 cm)

**Hydrangea (large)**
Flower: 6 × 6 in (15 × 15 cm)
Leaf: 3 × 3 in (7.5 × 7.5 cm)

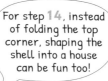

For step **14**, instead of folding the top corner, shaping the shell into a house can be fun too!

# Simple Maple Leaf

Photo on page 41

Make many with colorful paper and decorate for autumn!

Start from the Fish Base (page 16).

**1**

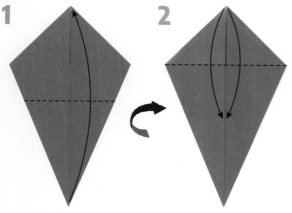

Fold the bottom corner of the upper layer to the top. Turn the paper over.

**2**

Fold the top flaps down along the dashed line.

**3**

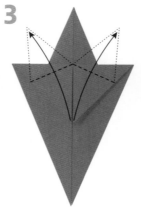

Fold the flaps back up diagonally.

**4**

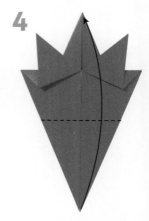

Fold the bottom corner to the top.

**5**

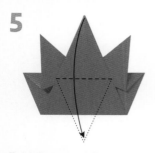

Fold the upper flap so that the corner sticks out a bit.

**6**

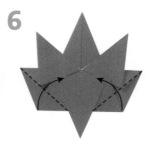

Fold in through both layers along the dashed lines. Turn the paper over.

*Finished!*

These are some of the autumn motifs introduced in another one of Kamikey's origami books. Have fun combining them in various ways!

From *Kamikey's Kawaii Seasonal Origami* (ISBN: 9784537218282) Acorn (page 98); Ginkgo Leaf (page 103); Squirrel (page 100)

**Simple Maple Leaf (page 41) size chart**

**Simple Maple Leaf (large)**
6 × 6 in
(15 × 15 cm)

**Simple Maple Leaf (small)**
3 × 3 in
(7.5 × 7.5 cm)

I'm a gorgeous dragonfly made using 3 sheets of origami paper.

## Body

Start by folding the paper in half vertically and horizontally to install creases.

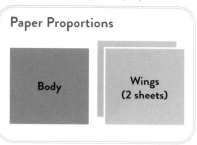

**Paper Proportions**

Body

Wings (2 sheets)

**1**

Fold the left and right corners to the center.

**2**

Fold the edges of the paper behind to meet at the center.

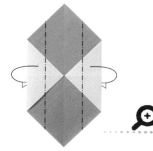

**3**

Open the white triangles to the left and right.

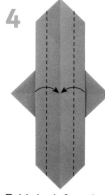

**4**

Fold the left and right upper layers to the center.

**5**

Make accordion folds as indicated.

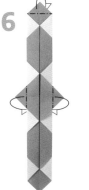

**6**

Fold the corners to the back.

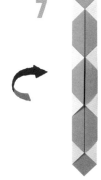

**7**

The Body is completed.

## Wings

Start after folding up to step **3** of the Cat's Head (page 27).

**1**

Open.

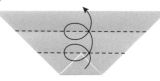

**2**

Fold along the dashed line as if rolling.

**3**

Fold the corners together.

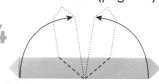

**4**

Fold as indicated.

**5**

The Wings are completed. Make two sets of these.

*Finished!*

Draw eyes on cut paper circles, or layer and apply large white and small black round stickers to create eyes. Glue the Wings to the Body.

47

# Bagworm
Photo on page 41

> I look cute hanging from a tree.

Start from the Square Base (page 15). Rotate the cut edges to face away from you.

**1**

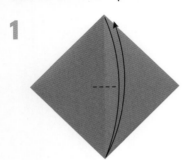

Fold the top layer in half but only place a short crease mark along the dashed line.

**2**

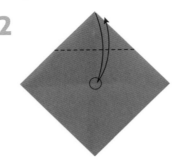

Fold the top layer to meet the circled location. Crease and unfold.

**3**

Fold inside along the crease made in step **2**. Repeat steps **1–3** for the back side as well.

**4**

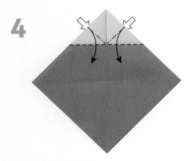

Open pockets at the 🖑🖐 symbols and flatten the flaps into squares.

**5**

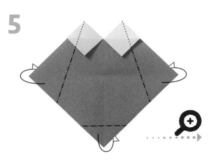

Fold to the back along the dashed lines (do not fold the white squares at the top).

**6**

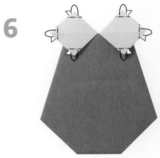

Fold the corners to the back.

### Tree and Bagworm (page 41) size chart

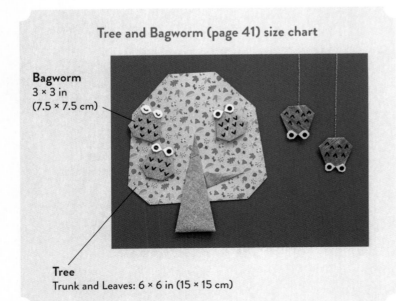

**Bagworm**
3 × 3 in
(7.5 × 7.5 cm)

**Tree**
Trunk and Leaves: 6 × 6 in (15 × 15 cm)

*Finished!*

Draw on the eyes and a pattern.

# Tree
Photo on page 41

## Trunk
Start from the Kite Base (page 16).

**Paper Proportions**

Trunk

Leaves

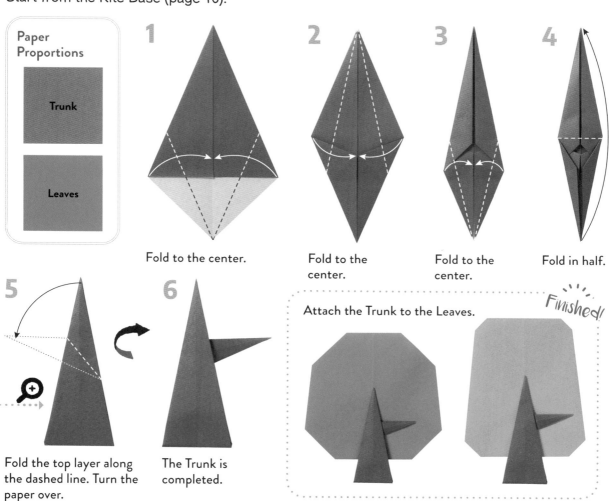

**1** Fold to the center.

**2** Fold to the center.

**3** Fold to the center.

**4** Fold in half.

**5** Fold the top layer along the dashed line. Turn the paper over.

**6** The Trunk is completed.

Attach the Trunk to the Leaves.

*Finished!*

## Leaves
Start by folding the paper in half vertically to install a crease.

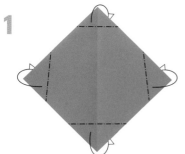

**1** Fold the corners to the back.

**2** The Leaves are completed.

By changing the width and angle of the corner folds, you can change the look of the tree canopy.

Make many Butterflies and connect them to create a beautiful wreath!

## Main body

Start by folding the paper in half vertically and horizontally to install creases.

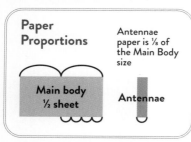

**Paper Proportions**

Antennae paper is ⅛ of the Main Body size

Main body ½ sheet

Antennae

*When making the Butterfly Wreath, prepare 8 sheets each of each type.*

**1**

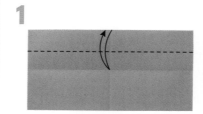

Fold the top edge to the center and unfold to create a crease.

**2**

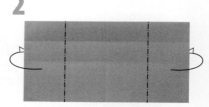

Fold the left and right sides behind to meet at the center.

**3**

Fold the corners behind to meet at the center.

**4**

Unfold everything.

**5**

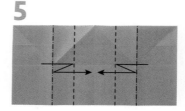

Grasp the existing mountain creases and accordion fold them to meet at the center.

**6**

Turn the paper over.

**7**

Fold in half.

**8**

Open pockets at the ⇧ symbols.

**9**

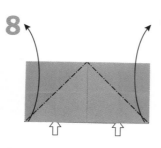

Flatten the inside and fold as shown in step **10**.

**10**

Pull down at the ● point, while folding the standing edges to the center.

**11**

Step **10** in progress.

**12**

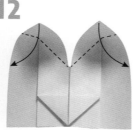

Fold the corners to meet the outer edge of the paper.

**13**

Step **12** in progress.

**14**

Fold along the dashed line.

Continues

**15**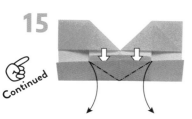

Open the pockets at the ⇩ symbols and flatten.

**16**

Turn it over.

**17**

The Main Body is completed.

## Antennae

**1**

Fold in half.

**2**

Fold in half.

**3**

Fold diagonally along the dashed line.

**4**

The Antennae are completed.

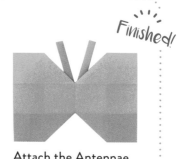

Finished!

Attach the Antennae to the back of the Main Body.

## Butterfly Wreath

**1**

Make 8 Butterflies, and then fold the bottom right corners to the back to install creases, unfolding after each.

If you make the Main Body with small paper (like 1½ × 3⅛ in / 4 × 8 cm) and attach it to a card, it makes a cute birthday card!

Happy Birthday

**2**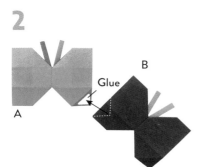

Glue

B

A

Align the edge of the paper on the bottom left of B with crease A made in step **1**, and then glue the Butterflies together.

**3**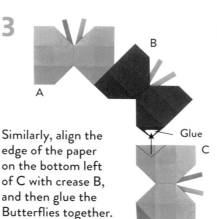

B

A

Glue

C

Similarly, align the edge of the paper on the bottom left of C with crease B, and then glue the Butterflies together.

Attach and connect the remaining 5 Butterflies in the same way to form a circle.

Finished!

51

# Zoo

These popular zoo superstars make wonderful interior decorations when displayed in a photo frame!

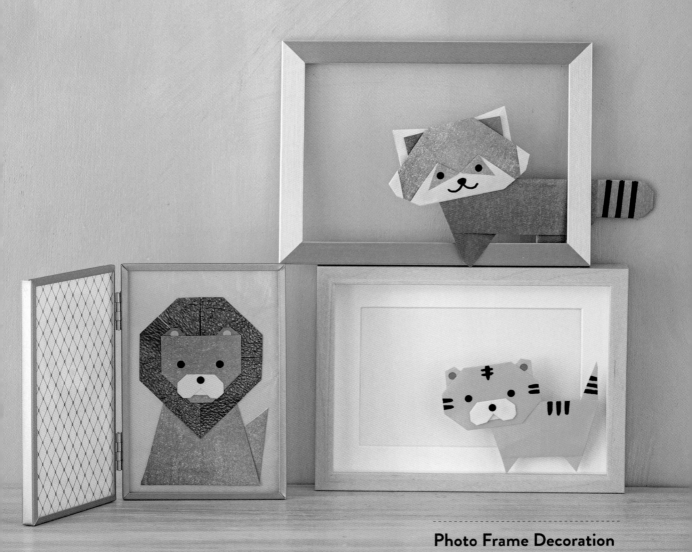

**Photo Frame Decoration**

Instructions on page 63

## Panda and Bamboo

Instructions on page 54 to 57

## Koala

Instructions on page 58

## Tiger

Instructions on page 63

# Panda in Profile

Photo on page 53

Depending on your mood, you can draw on the face, or attach an origami face!

## Head

Start by folding the paper in half vertically to install a crease.

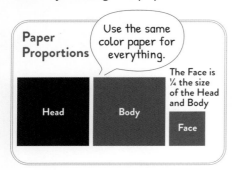

Paper Proportions

Use the same color paper for everything.

The Face is ¼ the size of the Head and Body

Head · Body · Face

**1**

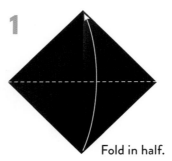

Fold in half.

**2**

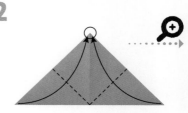

Fold the left and right corners to the circled corner.

**3**

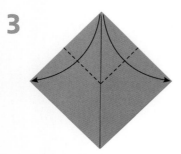

Fold the corners of the flaps from the top to the sides.

**4**

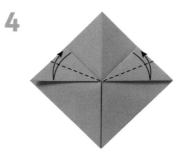

Bisect the angles to crease. Unfold.

**5**

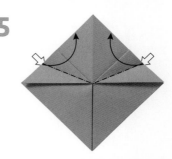

Open pockets at the ↘↙ symbols and flatten.

**6**

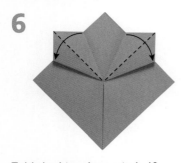

Fold the kite shapes in half.

**7**

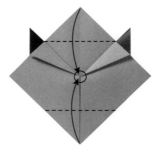

Fold the top and bottom corners to meet the circled location.

**8**

Fold in the corners. Turn the paper over.

**9**

The Head is completed. Draw on the face, or attach the Face part (opposite).

Finished!

Attach the Head to the Body.

# Face

Start by folding the paper in half vertically and horizontally to install creases.

**1**

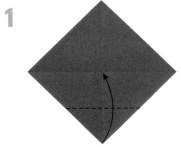

Fold the bottom corner to the center.

**2**

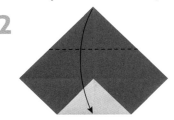

Fold the top corner to meet the bottom edge of the paper.

**3**

Fold in a small portion of the tip of the flap.

**4**

Fold the ★ corners behind to meet the circled location.

**5**

Fold the corners to the back.

**6**

The Face is completed.

# Body

Start by folding the paper in half vertically and horizontally to install creases.

**1**

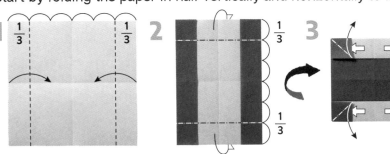

Fold as indicated, ⅓ of the distance to the center.

**2**

Fold behind as indicated, ⅓ of the distance to the center. Turn it over.

**3**

Open pockets at the ⇦ ⇨ symbols and flatten.

**4**

*If you fold it the other way from here, it will become a right-facing body.*

Fold behind as indicated.

**5**

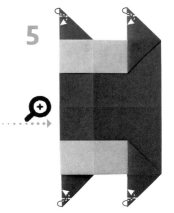

Make inside reverse folds as indicated.

**6**

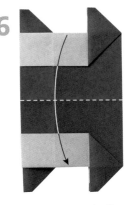

Fold the paper in half.

**7**

Accordion fold the corner to the back.

**8**

The Body is completed.

# Front-Facing Panda

Photo on page 53

By changing the body to face forward, you can make a front-facing panda!

## Body

Start from the Square Base (page 15). Start folding the base with the colored side facing up, and start folding the Body with the cut edges facing toward you.

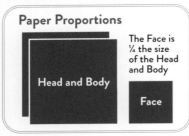

**Paper Proportions**

Head and Body

The Face is ¼ the size of the Head and Body

Face

*The methods for making the Head and Face are the same as for the Panda in Profile (page 54).*

**1**

Fold the top layer in half.

**2**

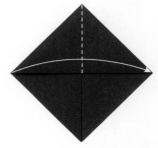

Fold the top flap along the dashed line, like turning a page.

**3**

Make it parallel to the vertical crease.

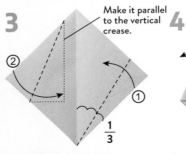

① Fold the top layer along the dashed line. ② Fold the flap along the dashed line.

**4**

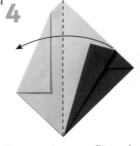

Return the part flipped in step **2**.

**5**

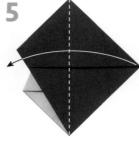

Flip the flap right to left, like turning a page.

**6**

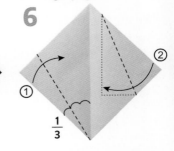

Fold step **3** in mirror image, then return the part flipped in step **5**.

**7**

Fold to the back as indicated. Turn the paper over.

**8**

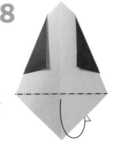

Fold the top layer inside as indicated, inserting it into the pocket.

**9**

Fold the flaps in half to the back.

Finished!

Attach the Head (page 54) to the Body.

**10**

Fold to the back as indicated.

**11**

The Body is completed.

## Part 1 — Bamboo

Photo on page 53

> Feel free to creatively adjust the direction of the branches and the number of leaves!

## Stalk

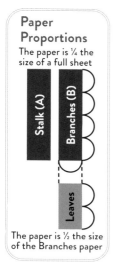

**Paper Proportions**

The paper is ¼ the size of a full sheet

Stalk (A)

Branches (B)

Leaves

The paper is ½ the size of the Branches paper

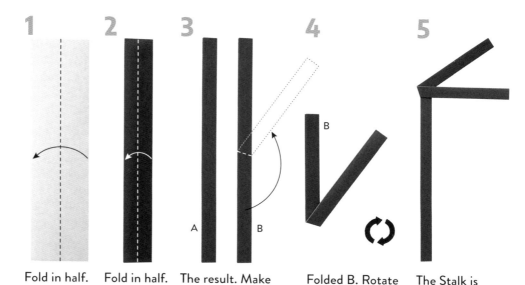

**1** Fold in half.

**2** Fold in half.

**3** The result. Make two of these, then fold B diagonally.

**4** Folded B. Rotate and attach to A.

**5** The Stalk is completed.

## Leaves

**1** Fold in half.

**2** Fold in half to create a crease. Unfold.

**3** Fold diagonally along the dashed line.

**4** Fold to the back at the indicated positions.

**5** The Leaves are completed. Make four of these.

**Sakura (page 117)**
3 × 3 in
(7.5 × 7.5 cm)

Thank You, Friend!

Let's stay fit and work hard!

Let's remain best friends!

> Write notes on the blossoms.

> A collection of messages featuring only Panda faces and colorful blossoms.

**Panda (Head) (page 54)**
Head: 4 × 4 in (10 × 10 cm)
Face: 2 × 2 in (5 × 5 cm)

**Colored paper**
Approx. 10⅝ × 9½
(27 × 24 cm)

*Finished!*

Attach the Leaves to the Branches.

# Koala

Photo on page 53

You can make a cute Koala hugging a tree!

## Body

Start by folding the paper in half vertically and horizontally to install creases.

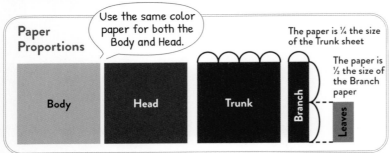

**Paper Proportions**

Use the same color paper for both the Body and Head.

Body | Head | Trunk | Branch | Leaves

The paper is ¼ the size of the Trunk sheet

The paper is ½ the size of the Branch paper

*The Branch and Leaves instructions are on page 57.*

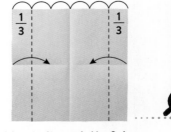

**1** Fold as indicated, ⅓ of the distance to the center.

$\frac{1}{3}$  $\frac{1}{3}$

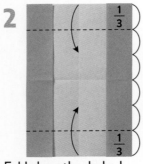

**2** Fold along the dashed lines.

$\frac{1}{3}$

$\frac{1}{3}$

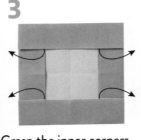

**3** Grasp the inner corners, pull them out, and fold them into triangular flaps.

**4** Step 3 in progress.

**5** Fold along the dashed line.

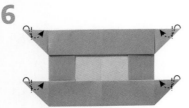

**6** Make inside reverse folds as indicated.

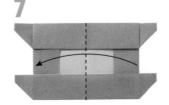

**7** Fold in half.

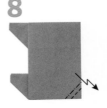

**8** Accordion fold to the back as indicated.

**9** The Body is completed.

## Trunk

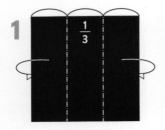

**1** Fold overlapping flaps to the back as indicated.

$\frac{1}{3}$

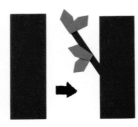

**2** The result. Attach the Branch—"Stalk (A)"—with Leaves from page 57 to the back of the Trunk.

Sandwich the Trunk with the Koala and secure with glue, then decorate.

*Finished!*

Attach the Head to the Body.

# Head

Start by folding the paper in half corner to corner both ways to install creases.

**1**

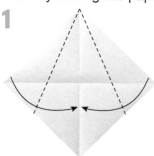

Fold to the center.

**2**

Fold to the back as indicated. Turn the paper over.

**3**

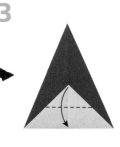

Fold the corner flap to meet the edge of the paper.

**4**

Fold the top corner to the point indicated by the circle.

**5**

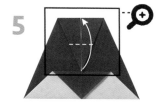

Fold the corner to meet the top edge. Steps **6–7** are detail views.

**6**

Fold a small portion of the corner to the back.

**7**

Fold the corners behind as indicated.

**8**

Turn the paper over.

**9**

Open the upper flaps and fold as indicated.

**10**

Fold down along the existing crease.

**11**

Fold slightly diagonally to the back. Turn the paper over.

**12**

Fold back along the dashed line.

**13**

Fold in along the dashed lines.

**14**

After folding along the dashed line, fold in mirror image to steps **12–13**, and then turn the paper over.

**15**

Fold the corners to the back to round the shape.

**16**

The Head is completed. Draw on the face.

Make smaller animals and attach them to bags or pouches as wrapping decorations!

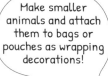

If you fold the Body (page 58) in the opposite direction from step **7** on, it will face to the right.

# Red Panda

Photo on page 52

The white edges of the ears and cheeks are also cutely expressed.

## Body

Start by folding the paper in half vertically and horizontally to install creases.

If you fold everything in the opposite direction from the start, it will face to the right.

Use the same color paper for both the Body and Head.

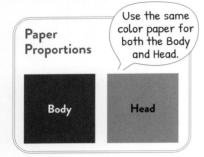

Paper Proportions

Body

Head

**1**

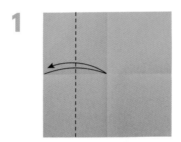

Fold the edge to the center to create a crease. Unfold.

**2**

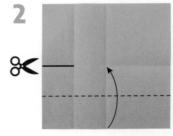

Cut along the span indicated by the bold line. Then, fold the bottom edge to the center.

**3**

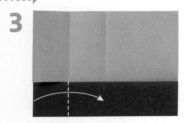

Fold the flap to the center.

**4**

Grasp the inner corner, pivot it down, and flatten it into a triangle.

**5**

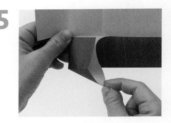

Step **4** in progress.

**6**

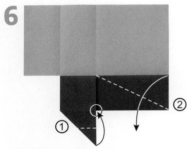

① Fold the corner to meet the circled location. ② Fold the top layer.

**7**

Fold along the dashed line.

**8**

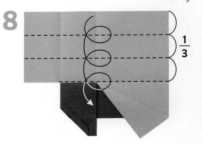

$\frac{1}{3}$

Fold along the dashed lines, as if rolling.

**9**

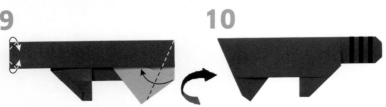

Fold in along the dashed lines and turn the paper over.

**10**

The Body is completed. Draw on the stripes on the tail.

Finished!

Attach the Head to the Body.

# Head

Start after folding up to step **2** of the Cat's Head (page 27).

**1**

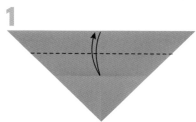

Fold the top edge of the paper to meet the horizontal crease and create a crease. Unfold.

**2**

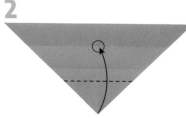

Fold one layer of the bottom corner to the circled location. Fold the back the same way.

**3**

Make sure to create a strong crease!

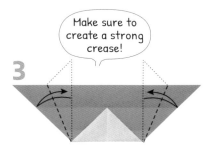

Fold along the dashed lines to install creases. Unfold.

**4**

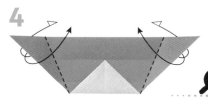

Inside reverse fold along the creases.

**5**

Fold along the dashed lines to install creases. Unfold.

**6**

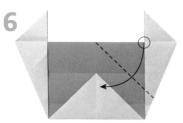

Fold to bring the circled location to the center.

**7**

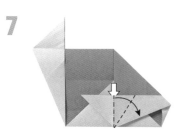

Open a pocket at the ⇩ symbol and bring the mountain fold line to the edge of the paper.

**8**

Step **7** in progress.

**9**

Fold the corners to meet the crease.

**10**

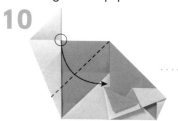

Fold the left side in the same way as steps **6–9**, but in the opposite direction.

**11**

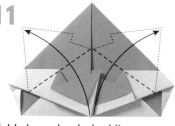

Fold along the dashed lines.

**12**

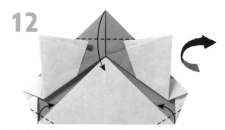

Fold the corners, and turn the paper over.

**13**

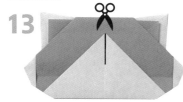

Cut only the top layer along the span indicated by the bold line.

**14**

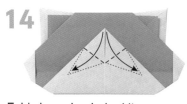

Fold along the dashed lines.

**15**

The Head is completed. Draw on the face.

61

# Lion

Photo on page 52

A majestic male lion with a splendid mane.

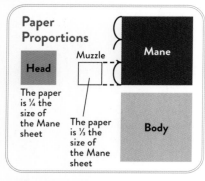

### Paper Proportions

**Head**

The paper is ¼ the size of the Mane sheet

**Muzzle**

The paper is ⅓ the size of the Mane sheet

**Mane**

**Body**

*Instructions for the Body: page 20.*
*Instructions for the Muzzle: page 22.*

## Mane

Start with the Blintz Base (page 16).

**1** Fold the corners behind to the center.

**2** Fold three corners and turn the paper over.

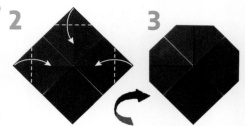

**3** The Mane is completed.

## Head

Start by folding in half vertically and horizontally to install creases.

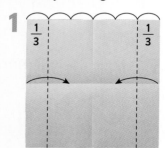

**1** Fold as indicated, ⅓ of the distance to the center.

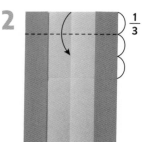

**2** Fold along the dashed line.

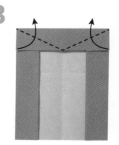

**3** Fold up the corners of the flap.

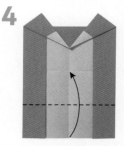

**4** Fold the bottom edge to meet the center.

**5** Fold the bottom corners to the edge of the flap.

**6** Fold down the corners and turn the paper over.

**7** The Head is completed.

## Assembly Instructions

Attach the Head to the Mane. Create the Muzzle (page 22), attach it to the Head, and draw on the face.

**Finished!**

Make the Body of the Shiba Inu (page 20) and attach the Head.

# Tiger

Photo on page 52

Draw on cool tiger stripes!

## Head

Start by folding vertically in half to install a crease.

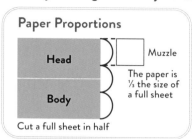

**Paper Proportions**

Head

Body

Cut a full sheet in half

Muzzle

The paper is ⅓ the size of a full sheet

*Instructions for the Muzzle: page 22.*
*Instructions for the Body: page 24*

**1**

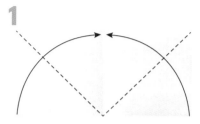

Fold the bottom edges to the center.

**2**

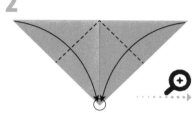

Fold the left and right corners to meet the bottom corner.

**3**

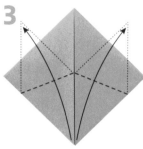

Fold the flaps along the dashed lines.

**4**

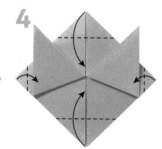

Fold the corners in.

**5**

Fold in the corners.

**6**

Fold in the corners, and turn the paper over.

**7**

The Head is completed. Attach the Muzzle (page 22) and draw on the face.

*Finished!*

Make the Body of the Chihuahua (page 24) and attach the Head.

**Photo Frame Decoration (page 52) size chart**

**Red Panda (page 60)**
Head and Body: 6 × 6 in (15 × 15 cm)

**Lion**
Mane and Body: 6 × 6 in (15 × 15 cm)
Head: 3 × 3 in (7.5 × 7.5 cm)
Muzzle: 2 × 2 in (5 × 5 cm)

**Tiger**
Head and Body:
3 × 6 in (7.5 × 15 cm)
Muzzle: 2 × 2 in (5 × 5 cm)

**Decorative Penguin Panel**

Instructions on page 70

# Aquarium

It's fun to make parents and children by gradually changing the sizes. Window decorations are also lovely.

## Seal

Instructions on page 73

## Polar Bear

Instructions on page 66

## Dolphin and Life Ring

Instructions on page 69

## Whale

Instructions on page 73

# Polar Bear

Photo on page 65

Photo on page 65

If you use brown paper, you can make a "regular" Bear too!

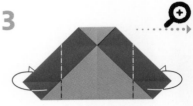

Start by folding corner to corner both ways to install creases.

**1**

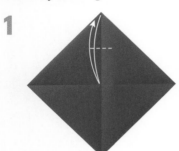

Bring the top corner to the center. Crease only on the dashed line, and unfold.

**2**

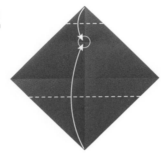

Fold the corners to meet the circled location.

**3**

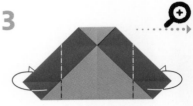

Fold the left and right corners behind to the center.

**4**

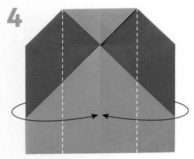

Fold the edges to the center, allowing the hidden flaps to swing out from behind.

**5**

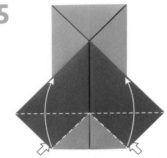

Open pockets at the ⤢⤡ symbols and flatten.

**6**

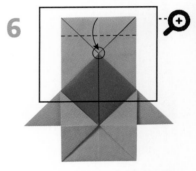

Fold the top edge of the paper to meet the circled location. Steps 7–9 show detail views.

**7**

Fold up the corners of the flap.

**8**

Fold in along the dashed lines.

**9**

Fold in the corners.

**10**

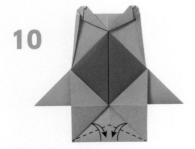

Fold along the dashed lines to install creases.

**11**

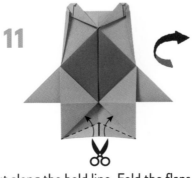

Cut along the bold line. Fold the flaps on the existing creases. Turn over.

*Finished!*

Draw on the face.

# Seal

Photo on page 65

Make a baby seal with a smaller piece of white paper.

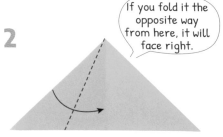

Start with the Waterbomb Base (page 17).

## Paper Proportions

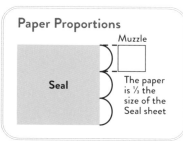

Muzzle

Seal

The paper is ⅓ the size of the Seal sheet

*Instructions for the Muzzle: page 22.*

**1**

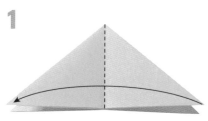

Flip the right flap along the dashed line, like turning a page.

**2**

If you fold it the opposite way from here, it will face right.

Fold the edge of the paper to the center.

**3**

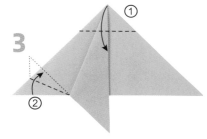

①
②

In step ①, fold down the corner. In step ②, fold the upper paper along the dashed line.

**4**

Bring the corner to meet the ● mark.

**5**

Fold a small portion of the corner and turn the paper over.

**6**

Fold along the dashed line.

**7**

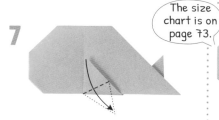

The size chart is on page 73.

Fold diagonally so that the corner sticks out.

**Finished!**

Make the Muzzle (page 22), attach it, and draw on the face.

## Polar Bear Pocket Pal

Start after folding up to step **2** of the Polar Bear.

**1**

Fold the lower triangular flap behind.

**2**

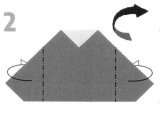

Fold and turn the paper over in the same way as steps **3–9** of the Polar Bear.

**3**

Tuck the flap inside along the dashed line.

**Finished!**

Draw on the face.

# Dolphin

Photo on page 65

Try making pink or white dolphins too!

Start by folding corner to corner both ways to install creases.

**1**

Fold the top right edge to align with the center.

**2**

If you fold it the opposite way from here, it will face right.

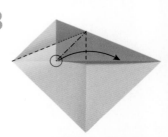

Make a crease by folding to align with the center. Unfold.

**3**

Grasp the circled corner, pivot it to the right, and flatten.

**4**

Step 3 in progress.

**5**

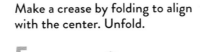

Fold the corner to align with the center.

**6**

Leave a small gap and fold behind.

Approximately ¼ in / 6 mm (for a 6 in / 15 cm square origami paper).

**7**

① ②

Fold backward along the dashed lines in the order of ①, then ② and turn it over.

**8**

Fold the corner to meet the center.

**9**

Fold back at about ¾ in (2 cm) from the edge of the paper.

¾ in (2 cm)

**10**

Fold a small portion of the corner and turn it over.

**11**

Fold along the dashed line to make a crease.

**12**

Outside reverse fold along the existing creases.

**13**

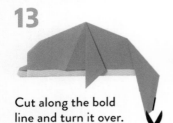

Cut along the bold line and turn it over.

**14**

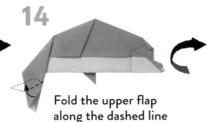

Fold the upper flap along the dashed line and turn it over.

Finished!

Draw on the eyes.

# Life Ring Wreath

Photo on page 65

If made small, it can be decorated together with the dolphin.

Prepare four pieces of paper of the same size.

**1**

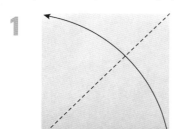

Fold in half.

**2**

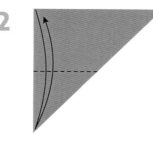

Fold to make a crease by aligning corner to corner. Unfold.

**3**

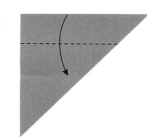

Fold the edge of the paper to align with the crease.

**4**

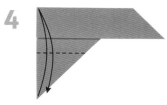

Fold to make a crease by aligning corner to corner.

**5**

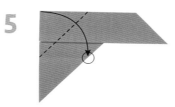

Fold the corner to meet the circled location.

**6**

The part is completed. Make four of the same.

Dolphin Ring (page 65) size chart

**Dolphin**
6 × 6 in (15 × 15 cm)

**Ring Wreath**
3 × 3 in (7.5 × 7.5 cm), 4 pieces

## Assembly Instructions

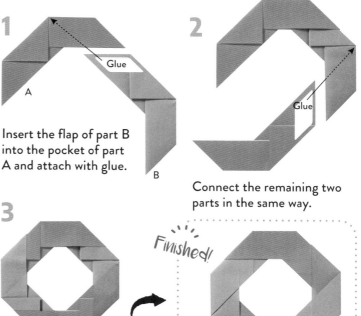

**1**

Glue

A

B

Insert the flap of part B into the pocket of part A and attach with glue.

**2**

Glue

Connect the remaining two parts in the same way.

**3**

The connected parts. Turn it over.

Finished!

# Penguin

Photo on page 64

## Head

Start with the Kite Base (page 16).

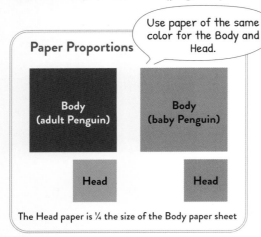

**Paper Proportions**

Use paper of the same color for the Body and Head.

Body (adult Penguin)

Body (baby Penguin)

Head

Head

The Head paper is ¼ the size of the Body paper sheet

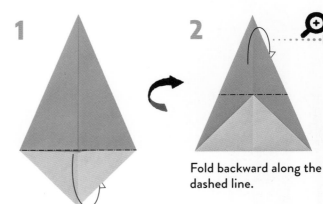

**1**

Fold backward along the dashed line and turn it over.

**2**

Fold backward along the dashed line.

**3**

Fold the corner to meet the circled location.

**4**

Fold a small portion of the corner.

**5**

Fold backward along the dashed lines.

**6**

The Head is completed. Draw on the eyes and color the beak.

**From *Kamikey's Kawaii Seasonal Origami* (ISBN: 9784537218282)**
Penguin Envelope (page 76)

Other Kamikey books also introduce origami models featuring this popular animal. Try using them together to decorate!

**From *Kamikey's Seasonal Origami* (ISBN: 9784537216417)**
Penguin Box (page 70)

**Decorative Penguin Panel (page 64) size chart**

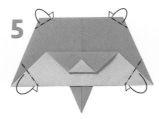

**Starfish (page 117)**
3 × 3 in
(7.5 × 7.5 cm)

**Shell (page 80)**
3 × 3 in
(7.5 × 7.5 cm)

**Adult Penguin - Small**
**Baby Penguin**
Body: 4¾ × 4¾ in
(12 × 12 cm)
Head: 2 × 2 in
(5 × 5 cm)

**Adult Penguin - Large**
Body: 6 × 6 in
(15 × 15 cm)
Head: 3 × 3 in
(7.5 × 7.5 cm)

## Adult Penguin's Body

Start from the Square Base (page 15). Start folding the base with the colored side facing up, and start folding the Body with the cut edges facing toward you.

**1**

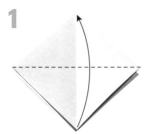

Fold the top layer in half. Do the same for the back.

**2**

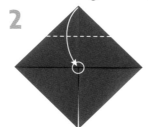

Fold the top layer's corner to meet the circled location.

**3**

Unfold what was folded in step **1**.

**4**

Fold the top layer inside along the dashed lines.

**5**

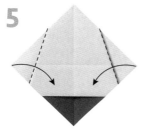

Fold along the dashed lines.

**6**

Fold the flaps behind along the dashed lines.

**7**

The Adult Penguin's Body is completed.

## Assembly Instructions

Insert the Body into the pocket of the Head and glue it. Do the same for the Baby Penguin.

## Baby Penguin's Body

Start from the Square Base (page 15). Start folding the Body with the cut edges facing toward you.

**1**

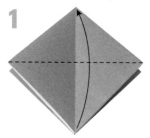

Fold the top layer in half. Do the same for the back.

**2**

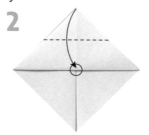

Fold both the front and back as in steps **2–3** of the Adult Penguin's Body, and also fold steps **4–6**.

**3**

The Baby Penguin's Body is completed.

If you put a small Santa hat on it, it instantly creates a Christmas atmosphere! Glue it on postcard-size paper to make a Christmas card.

**Postcard**
Approximately
6 × 4 in (15 × 10 cm)

**Santa Hat (page 137)**
2 × 2 in
(5 × 5 cm)

**Penguin**
Body: 4¾ × 4¾ in
(12 × 12 cm)
Head: 2 × 2 in
(5 × 5 cm)

Finished!

This is a fun project with a spout.

## Body

### Paper Proportions

Body

Half of the vertical size of the Body, divided by ¼.

Spout

**1**

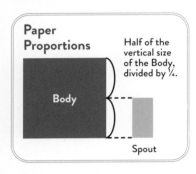

Fold in half.

**2**

If you fold it the opposite way from here, it will face right.

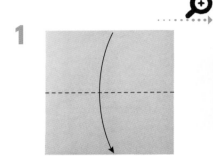

Fold in half.

**3**

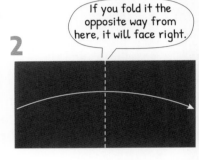

Open the pocket from the ⇦ symbol and flatten.

**4**

Flip the flap right to left, like turning a page.

**5**

Fold the left corner to the center. Crease and unfold.

**6**

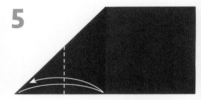

Fold to align ○ and ○.

**7**

Fold the top layer along the dashed line.

**8**

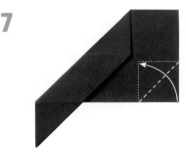

Turn the paper over.

**9**

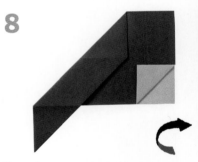

Fold the top layer to align with the corner of the underlying paper (indicated by the ○ mark).

**10**

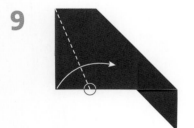

Tuck the flap folded in step **9** inside.

**11**

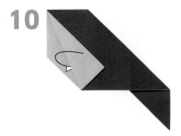

Continues

Fold the flaps together along the dashed line.

**12**

Fold the upper layer to bisect the angle.

**13**

Fold behind along the dashed line. Rotate the paper.

**14**

The Body is completed. Draw on the eyes.

---

# Spout

**1**

Fold in half.

**2**

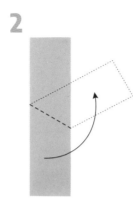

Fold diagonally along the dashed line.

**3**

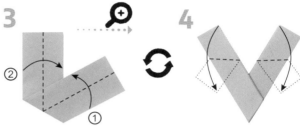

Fold along the dashed lines in the order of ①, then ②. Rotate the paper.

**4**

Fold along the dashed lines.

**5**

Turn the paper over.

**6**

The Spout is completed.

---

### Seal & Whale (page 65) size chart

**Seal (small)—page 67**
Body: 4¾ × 4¾ in (12 × 12 cm)
Muzzle: 1½ × 1½ in (3.75 × 3.75 cm)

**Whale (small)**
3 × 3 in (7.5 × 7.5 cm)

**Seal (large)**
Main body: 6 × 6 in (15 × 15 cm)
Muzzle: 2 × 2 in (5 × 5 cm)

**Whale (large)**
Body: 6 × 6 in (15 × 15 cm)
Spout: 3 × 1½ in (7.5 × 3.75 cm)

*Finished!*

Attach the Spout to the back of the Body.

# Small Sea Creatures

Colorful fish and shells look vibrant when folded with gradient paper. Even small paper creations glued on a card or arranged in a row are cute.

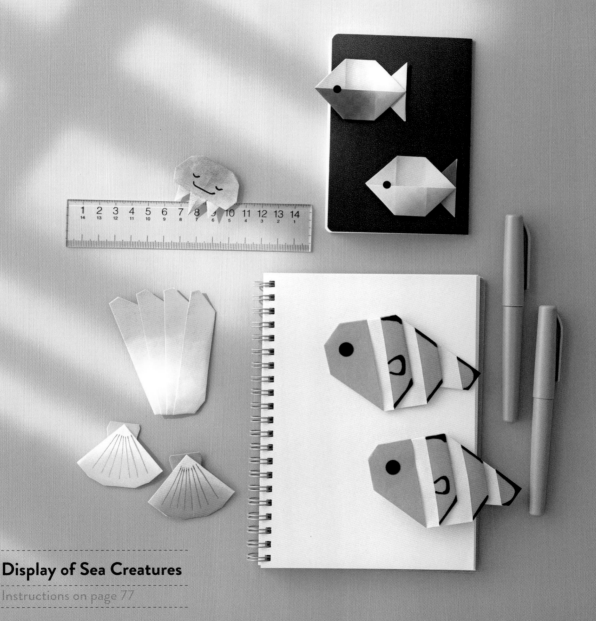

**Display of Sea Creatures**

Instructions on page 77

74

## Jellyfish

Instructions on page 77

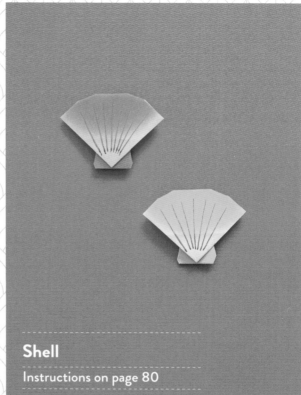

## Shell

Instructions on page 80

## Crab

Instructions on page 77

## Bicolor Fish

Instructions on page 78

# Clownfish

Photo on page 74

I designed this model with the three characteristic white stripes of the clownfish!

Start with the Waterbomb Base (page 17) Start folding the base with the colored side facing up.

**1**

Unfold everything to reveal the white side.

**2**

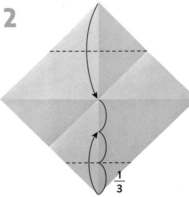

$\frac{1}{3}$

Fold along the dashed lines.

**3**

If you fold it the opposite way from here, it will face right.

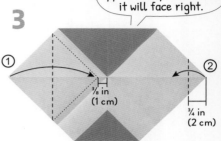

① ②

³⁄₈ in (1 cm)

¾ in (2 cm)

In step ①, fold the corner about ³⁄₈ in (1 cm) short of the center. In step ②, fold over about a ¾ in (2 cm) flap.

**4**

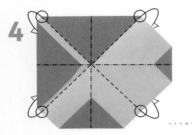

Gather the four corners to the back, collapsing the paper.

**5**

The collapse in progress. Tilt the ★ corners to the left and right.

**6**

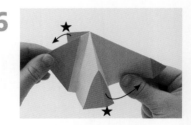

Tilting the ★ corners to the left and right.

**7**

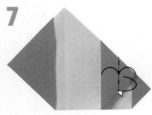

Fold the corner in half, tucking it inside.

**8**

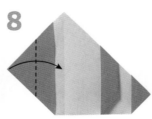

Fold the top layer of the left corner of the paper to align with the crease.

**9**

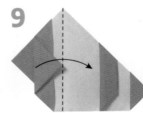

Use the existing crease to flip the flap to the right.

**10**

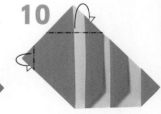

Fold behind along the dashed lines.

**11**

Do not fold this part of the top paper.

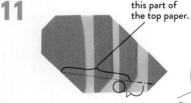

Fold the paper under the portion indicated by the ○ behind.

View from the back.

Finished!

Draw on the eyes and fins.

# Sea Anemone

Photo on page 74

Create ocean decorations along with fish and shells.

Start with the Waterbomb Base (page 17).

**1**

Flip the flap left to right, like turning a page.

**2**

Fold the upper layer slightly diagonally.

**3**

Fold the next layer shifted slightly more diagonally than the step **2** layer.

**4**

Fold the last layer shifted slightly more diagonally than the step **3** layer.

**5**

Fold behind along the dashed lines.

**6**

Fold small portions of the corners behind.

Finished!

## Display of Sea Creatures (page 74) size chart

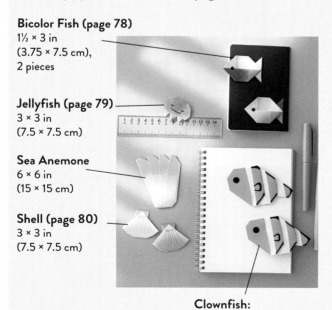

**Bicolor Fish (page 78)**
1½ × 3 in
(3.75 × 7.5 cm),
2 pieces

**Jellyfish (page 79)**
3 × 3 in
(7.5 × 7.5 cm)

**Sea Anemone**
6 × 6 in
(15 × 15 cm)

**Shell (page 80)**
3 × 3 in
(7.5 × 7.5 cm)

**Clownfish:**
6 × 6 in (15 × 15 cm)

## Jellyfish & Crab (page 75) size chart

**Jellyfish (large)**
—page 79
6 × 6 in
(15 × 15 cm)

**Jellyfish (small)**
3 × 3 in
(7.5 × 7.5 cm)

**Crab (small)**
—page 81
4 × 4 in
(10 × 10 cm)

**Crab (large)**
6 × 6 in
(15 × 15 cm)

# Bicolor Fish

Photo on page 74

## Part A

Start by folding in half to install a vertical crease.

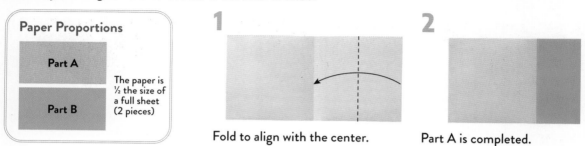

| | |
|---|---|
| **Paper Proportions** | |
| Part A | The paper is ½ the size of a full sheet (2 pieces) |
| Part B | |

**1** Fold to align with the center.

**2** Part A is completed.

## Part B

Start by folding in half to install a vertical crease.

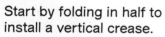

**1** Fold in half bottom to top.

**2** Fold the right edge to the center.

**3** Open the pocket from the ⇩ symbol and flatten.

**4** Turn it over.

**5** Part B is completed.

## Assembly Instructions

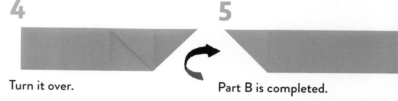

**1** Insert Part A into the front pocket of Part B.

A

B

**2** Fold the corners to align with the top edge of Part B.

**3** Fold the corner to meet the circled location while pulling out the back paper.

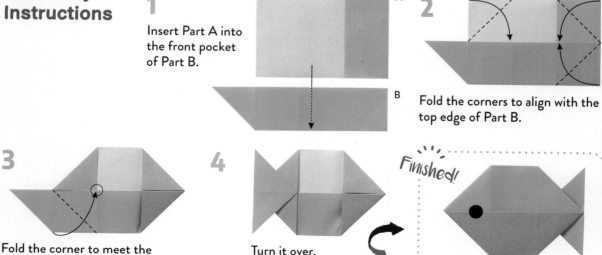

**4** Turn it over.

*Finished!*

Draw on the eyes.

# Jellyfish

Photo on page 75

It's also lovely if made with tracing paper or cellophane.

Start with the Fish Base (page 16).

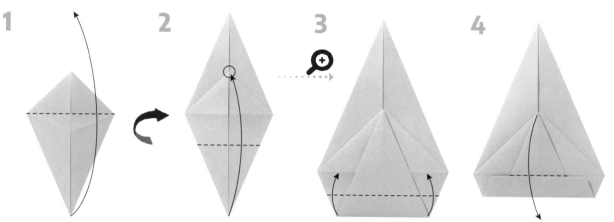

**1** Fold the flap along the dashed line. Turn the paper over.

**2** Fold the bottom corner to meet the circled location.

**3** Fold the edge of the paper to align with the crease.

**4** Fold the uppermost flap down along the dashed line.

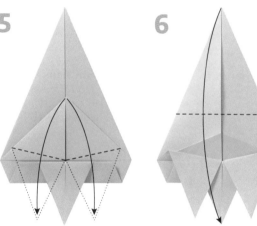

**5** Fold down the flaps diagonally.

**6** Fold to align corner to corner.

**7** Fold in small portions of the corners. Turn the paper over.

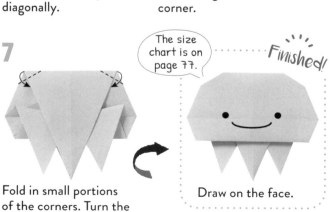

The size chart is on page 77.

Finished!

Draw on the face.

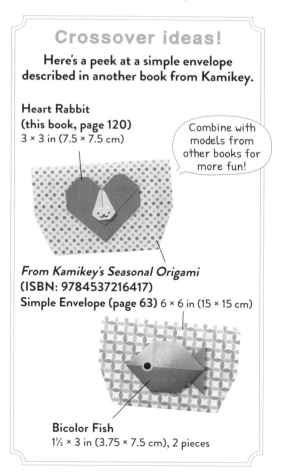

## Crossover ideas!

Here's a peek at a simple envelope described in another book from Kamikey.

**Heart Rabbit (this book, page 120)** 3 × 3 in (7.5 × 7.5 cm)

Combine with models from other books for more fun!

*From Kamikey's Seasonal Origami* (ISBN: 9784537216417) **Simple Envelope (page 63)** 6 × 6 in (15 × 15 cm)

**Bicolor Fish** 1½ × 3 in (3.75 × 7.5 cm), 2 pieces

It's cute when made with smaller paper and used as decoration!

Start by folding up to step **9** of the Crane Base (page 15).

**1**

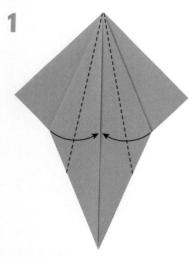

Fold the sides of the top layer to align with the center.

**2**

Fold through all layers at the top. Turn the paper over.

**3**

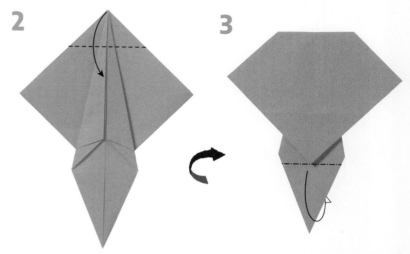

Fold backward along the dashed line.

**4**

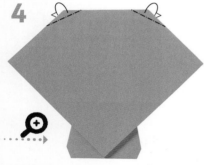

Fold small portions of the corners backward.

Finished!

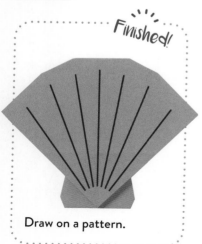

Draw on a pattern.

## Crossover ideas!

**More undersea friends from another book from Kamikey.**

From *Kamikey's Heartfelt Gift Origami* (ISBN: 9784537219517): Constellation Girls (pages 25, 33)

Pisces

Cancer

Starfish (this book, page 117)

From *Kamikey's Kawaii Seasonal Origami* (ISBN: 9784537218282): Telescope Goldfish (page 82) 3 × 3 in (7.5 × 7.5 cm)

Try decorating with models from other Kamikey books!

Sending Summer Greetings

Postcard Approximately 6 × 4 in (15 × 10 cm)

# Crab

Photo on page 75

 Try different facial expressions!

Start with the Kite Base (page 16).

**1**

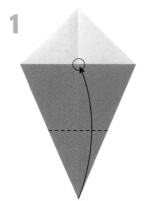

Fold the corner to meet the circled location.

**2**

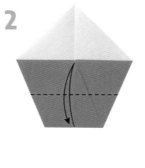

Align the edges of the paper and make a crease.

**3**

Return to the shape in step **1**.

**4**

Fold along the dashed line.

**5**

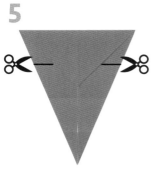

Cut along the bold lines.

**6**

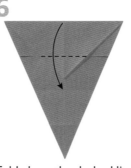

Fold along the dashed line.

**7**

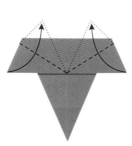

Fold up the corners of the flap.

**8**

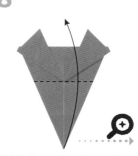

Fold along the dashed line.

**9**

Fold backward along the dashed line and turn it over.

**10**

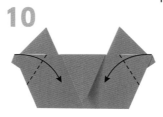

Fold in the corner flaps.

**11**

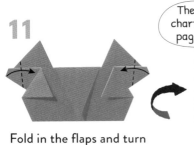

Fold in the flaps and turn it over.

The size chart is on page 77.

*Finished!*

Draw on the face.

A refreshing summer greeting card decorated with sea creatures.

**Postcard**
Approximately
6 × 4 in
(15 × 10 cm)

**Crab**
4 × 4 in
(10 × 10 cm)

**Shell**
2 × 2 in
(5 × 5 cm)

# Animal Cosplay

Adding ears, wings and a tail to paper figurines turns them into delightful animal cosplay characters!

The cute, rounded forms of Ladybug and Bumblebee Boys will also create a fun atmosphere in wreaths and other decorations.

**Butterfly Girl's Welcome Sign**

Instructions on page 91

**Butterfly Girl**

Instructions on page 91

**Ladybug Boy**

Instructions on page 88

let's go!

# Hello!

**Bumblebee Boy**

Instructions on page 90

**Rabbit Cosplay**

Instructions on page 87

waku waku

doki doki

**Cat Cosplay**

Instructions on page 86

By adding ears and tails, you can create various animal costumes.

## Head

Start by folding corner to corner both ways to install creases.

**Paper Proportions**

The Head paper is ¼ the size of the Body

Head

Body

**1** Fold the corner to align with the center.

**2** Fold the corners to align with the center.

**3** Turn the paper over.

**4** Fold the corners to meet at the circled location.

**5** Fold along the dashed lines.

**6** Open the pockets at the ☝ ☝ symbols and flatten.

**7** Turn it over.

**8** The Head is completed. Draw on the face.

Attach ears, tail and wings from pages 86–87 and 90–91 to enjoy animal cosplay!

Finished!

Attach the Head to the Body.

# Body

Start with the Waterbomb Base (page 17).

**1**

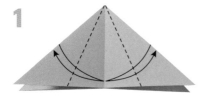

Fold the edges of the upper flaps to align with the center to make creases. Unfold.

**2**

Open the pocket at the ⇧ symbol and flatten.

**3**

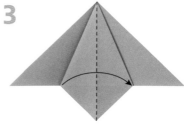

Flip the flap left to right along the dashed line, like turning a page.

**4**

Fold the left side in mirror image to steps **2**–**3**.

**5**

Fold the ★ corners along with the underlying paper to meet at the circled location.

**6**

Fold the edge of the flaps to meet the circled locations.

**7**

Return to the shape in step **5**.

**8**

Inside reverse fold along the dashed lines.

**9**

Fold along the existing creases.

**10**

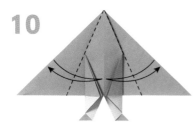

Fold along the dashed lines to make creases. Unfold.

**11**

Fold along the dashed lines.

**12**

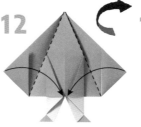

Fold along the existing creases and turn it over.

**13**

The Body is completed.

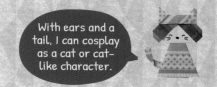

With ears and a tail, I can cosplay as a cat or cat-like character.

## Cat Ears

Start by folding vertically in half to install a crease.

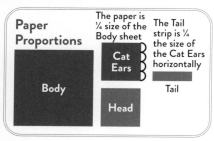

| Paper Proportions | The paper is ¼ size of the Body sheet | The Tail strip is ¼ the size of the Cat Ears horizontally |
|---|---|---|
| Body | Cat Ears | Tail |
| | Head | |

*The Body and Head are from Dress-Up Girl (pages 84–85)*

**1**

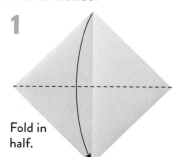

Fold in half.

**2**

Fold the left and right corners to meet the circled location.

**3**

Open the pockets at the ▷ ◁ symbols and flatten.

**4**

Turn the paper over.

**5**

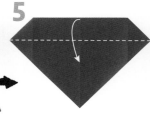

Bring forward the flattened squares while folding along the dashed line.

**6**

Fold backward along the dashed lines.

**7**

The Cat Ears are completed.

### Tiger Ears

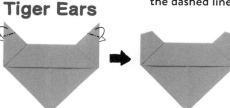

Fold small portions of the Cat Ears corners backward to make "Tiger Girl" or "Leopard Girl" ears.

### Assembly Instructions

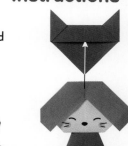

## Tail

**1**

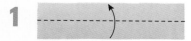

Fold in half.

**2**

If you fold it the opposite way from here, the tail will be attached to the right.

Fold diagonally.

**3**

Fold backward along the dashed lines.

**4**

The Tail is completed.

Continues

Insert the Dress-Up Girl (page 84) into the pocket of the Cat Ears and attach the Tail at the back.

# Rabbit Cosplay

Photo on page 83

Adding ears to a Dress-Up Girl makes a cute bunny cosplay!

## Bunny Ears

Start by folding vertically in half to install a crease.

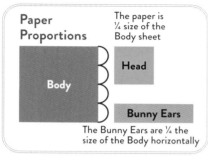

**Paper Proportions**

The paper is ¼ size of the Body sheet

Body

Head

Bunny Ears

The Bunny Ears are ¼ the size of the Body horizontally

*The Body and Head are from Dress-Up Girl (pages 84–85)*

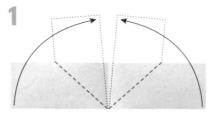

**1** Fold slightly diagonally to create a gap.

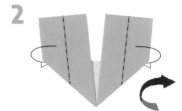

**2** Fold the pink parts in half to the rear and turn it over.

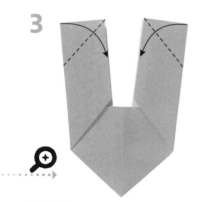

**3** Fold the corners to align with the edges of the paper.

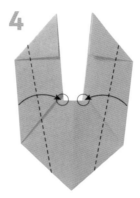

**4** Fold along the dashed lines.

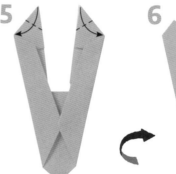

**5** Fold down the corners and turn it over.

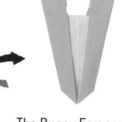

**6** The Bunny Ears are completed.

Continued

Finished!

Draw a pattern on the ears and body for a "Tiger Girl" or "Leopard Girl."

Finished!

Make a Dress-Up Girl (page 84) and attach the Bunny Ears to the back of the head.

# Ladybug Boy

Photo on page 83

The round form makes this Ladybug Boy cute!

## Body

Start by folding vertically in half to install a crease.

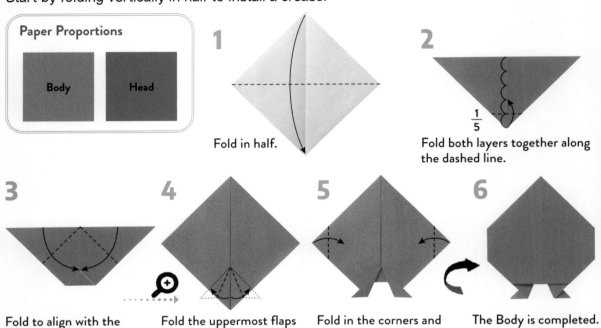

**Paper Proportions**

Body | Head

**1**
Fold in half.

**2**
$\frac{1}{5}$
Fold both layers together along the dashed line.

**3**
Fold to align with the center.

**4**
Fold the uppermost flaps along the dashed lines.

**5**
Fold in the corners and turn it over.

**6**
The Body is completed.

### Crossover ideas!

**Notebook Birthday Card from another Kamikey book**

**Hamster (this book, page 30)**
3 × 3 in (7.5 × 7.5 cm)

Combine with origami from other books for more fun!

Happy Birthday

Glue your favorite animal inside and write a message!

From *Kamikey's Heartfelt Gift Origami* (ISBN: 9784537219517):
**Notebook (page 91)**
Cover 10 × 10 in (26 × 26 cm)
Pages: 3¾ × 14 in (9.5 × 36 cm)

**Flower (this book, page 117)**
2 × 2 in (5 × 5 cm)

1 in (2.5 cm)    1 in (2.5 cm)

Fold the "pages" using the long side of A4 paper, as shown in the diagram.

2 in (5 cm)

Insert the Body into the pocket of the Head.

Finished!

Draw on the pattern.

# Head

Start by folding up through step **9** of the Crane Base (page 15).

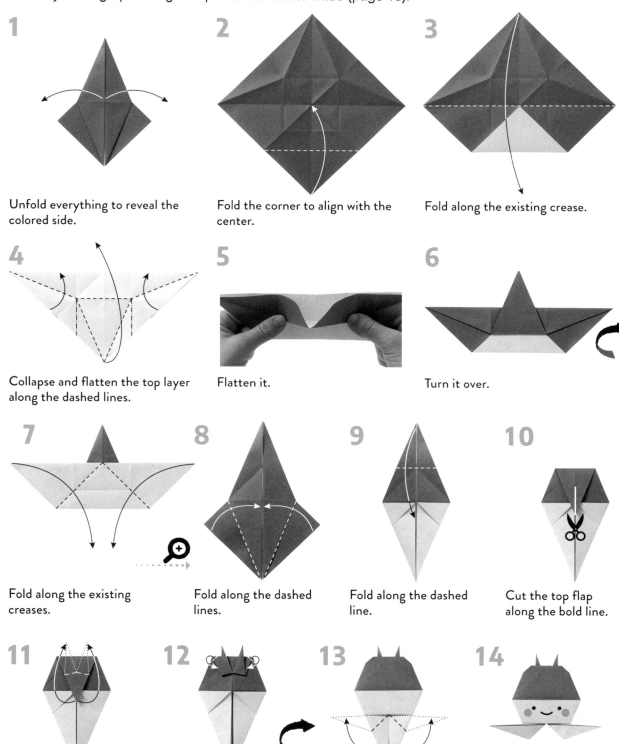

**1**

Unfold everything to reveal the colored side.

**2**

Fold the corner to align with the center.

**3**

Fold along the existing crease.

**4**

Collapse and flatten the top layer along the dashed lines.

**5**

Flatten it.

**6**

Turn it over.

**7**

Fold along the existing creases.

**8**

Fold along the dashed lines.

**9**

Fold along the dashed line.

**10**

Cut the top flap along the bold line.

**11**

Fold small portions of the flaps diagonally.

**12**

Fold small portions of the corners and turn it over.

**13**

Fold the flaps to either side along the dashed lines.

**14**

The Head is completed. Draw on the face.

# Bumblebee Boy

Photo on page 83

By making a little tweak to the Ladybug Boy, he becomes a Bumblebee Boy!

## Body

Start by folding through step **4** of the Ladybug Boy Body (page 88).

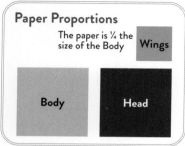

**Paper Proportions**

The paper is ¼ the size of the Body

Wings

Body

Head

*The Head instructions are on page 89*

**1**

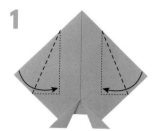

Fold along the dashed lines.

**2**

Turn it over.

**3**

The Body is completed.

## Wings

Start by folding corner to corner both ways to install creases.

**1**

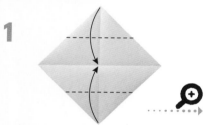

Fold the corners to meet at the center.

**2**

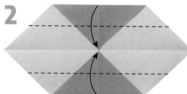

Fold the edges to meet at the center.

**3**

Fold in half.

**4**

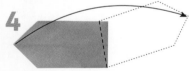

Fold the uppermost flap slightly diagonally, forming a crimp.

**5**

Fold in small portions of the corners and turn it over.

**6**

The Wings are completed.

Glue the Bumblebee Boy onto a hexagonal paper to make a cute door name plate.

**Hexagon board**
Bottom: 5½ × 5½ in (14 × 14 cm) (use thick paper)
Top: 4½ × 4½ in (11.5 × 11.5 cm)

**Bumblebee Boy**
Body and Head: 6 × 6 in (15 × 15 cm)
Wings: 3 × 3 in (7.5 × 7.5 cm)

Make the Ladybug Boy's Head (page 89), insert the Body, and attach the Wings at the back.

*Finished!*

Draw on the pattern.

**Part 1 Butterfly Girl**

Photo on page 82

 It's also lovely to make the body and wings with patterned paper.

## Wings

Start by folding through step **1** of the Bumblebee Boy Wings (page 90).

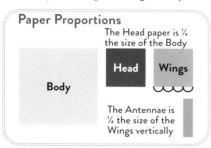

**Paper Proportions**

The Head paper is ¼ the size of the Body

Body

Head

Wings

The Antennae is ¼ the size of the Wings vertically

*The Body and Head are on pages 84–85. The Antennae is on page 51.*

**1**

Fold the top edge to meet the center.

**2**

Fold in half.

**3**

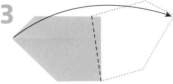

Fold the uppermost flap slightly diagonally, forming a crimp.

**4**

Fold in small portions of the corners and turn it over.

**5**

The Wings are completed.

*Finished!*

Make the Antennae (page 51) and attach it to the back of the Dress-Up Girl's Head (page 84). Attach the Wings to the back of the Body.

If you make the Wings like the Bumblebee Boy's Wings (page 90), she becomes Bumblebee Girl!

**Butterfly Girl's Welcome Sign (page 82) size chart**

The "cosplay kids" introduced together on page 83 can be made in any size you like.

**Base Paper**
5 × 10½ in (13.5 × 27 cm)

**Flower (medium)**
2 × 2 in (5 × 5 cm)

**Butterfly Girl**
Body: 6 × 6 in (15 × 15 cm)
Head and wings: 3 × 3 in (7.5 × 7.5 cm)
Antennae: 3 × ¾ in (7.5 × 2 cm)

**Flower (small)**
2 × 2 in (5 × 5 cm)

**Flower (large) (page 117)**
3 × 3 in (7.5 × 7.5 cm)

# Part 2

Small Animal Items

# Pocket Items

Animals with pockets and envelopes that can hold shared treats, souvenirs and small items. Attach a heartfelt message!

## Square Envelope

Instructions on page 101

## Cat Gum Holder

Instructions on page 97

## Frog Toothpick Holder

Instructions on page 96

## Halloween Pocket Items

Instructions on page 98 – 100

Congratulations

## Message Animal

Instructions on page 94

Nice to
Meet You

Thank You

It looks like they're holding the message with both hands!

Thank You · Congratulations · Nice to Meet You

## Rabbit

Start by folding vertically and horizontally in half to install creases.

**1**

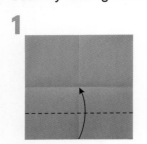

Fold the bottom edge to the center.

**2**

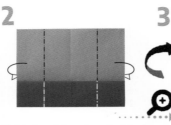

Fold the side edges behind to the center, and turn the paper over.

**3**

Fold the flaps in half along the dashed lines.

**4**

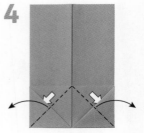

Open pockets at the ✎ ✎ symbols and flatten.

**5**

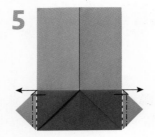

Valley and mountain fold along the dashed lines.

**6**

Fold backward along the dashed lines.

**7**

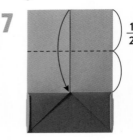

$\frac{1}{2}$

Fold along the dashed line.

**8**

Fold the uppermost flap along the dashed lines.

**9**

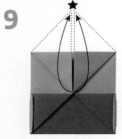

Grasp the top corners of the flaps and pull them out to the ★ mark.

**10**

Step **9** in progress.

**11**

Fold along the dashed lines, and turn the paper over.

Finished!

Draw on the face.

## Dog

Start by folding up through step **10** of the Rabbit.

**1**

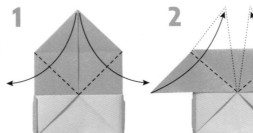

Fold the flaps along the dashed lines.

**2**

Fold the flaps slightly diagonally.

**3**

Continues

Fold along the dashed lines, and turn it over.

# Monkey Face

Start with the Kite Base (page 16).

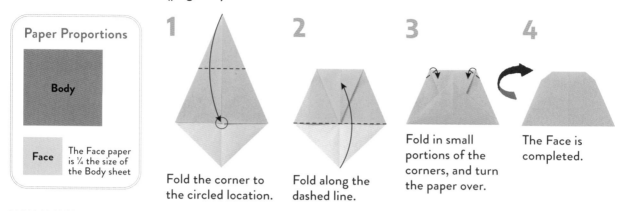

**Paper Proportions**

**Body**

**Face** The Face paper is ¼ the size of the Body sheet

**1** Fold the corner to the circled location.

**2** Fold along the dashed line.

**3** Fold in small portions of the corners, and turn the paper over.

**4** The Face is completed.

# Body

Start by folding up through step **10** of the Rabbit.

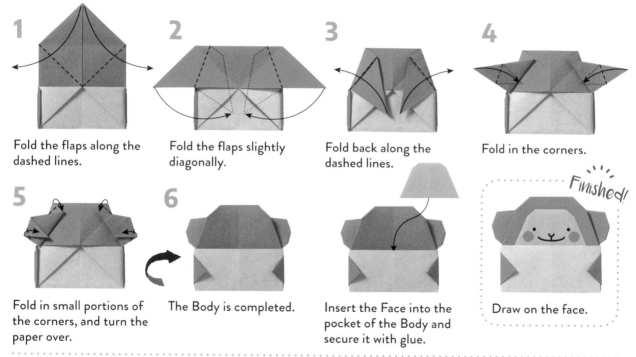

**1** Fold the flaps along the dashed lines.

**2** Fold the flaps slightly diagonally.

**3** Fold back along the dashed lines.

**4** Fold in the corners.

**5** Fold in small portions of the corners, and turn the paper over.

**6** The Body is completed.

Insert the Face into the pocket of the Body and secure it with glue.

**Finished!**

Draw on the face.

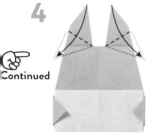

**4** Fold along the dashed lines.

**5** Fold backward along the dashed lines.

**Continued**

**Finished!**

Draw on the face.

95

# Frog Toothpick Holder

Photo on page 92

Very convenient when going out!

Start with the Blintz Base (page 16).

**1**

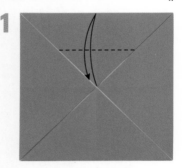

Fold the corner of the flap to the top edge. Crease and unfold.

**2**

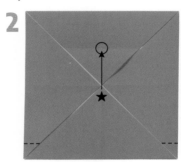

Shift the ★ corner up to meet the circled location.

**3**

Fold the corner inside to meet the circled location.

**4**

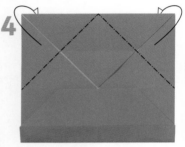

Fold the corners behind along the dashed lines, and turn it over.

**5**

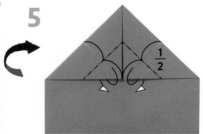

Fold the flaps inside along the dashed lines. Crease and unfold.

**6**

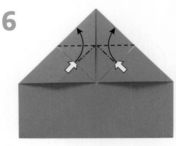

Open pockets at the ↗↘ symbols and flatten.

**7**

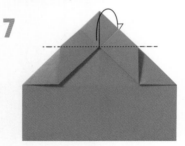

Fold the underlying flap around to the back.

**8**

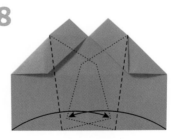

Fold so that the left and right corners overlap.

**9**

Fold in small portions of the corners, and turn it over.

Lift the face and insert a few toothpicks.

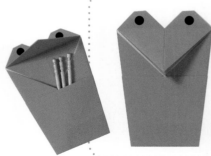

Finished!

Draw on the eyes.

# Cat Gum Holder

Photo on page 92

Great for a little sharing!

## Head

Start by folding vertically and horizontally in half to install creases.

**1**

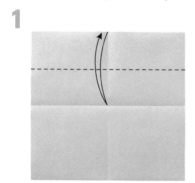

Fold the top edge to the center. Crease and unfold.

**2**

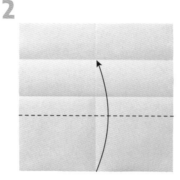

Fold the bottom edge of the paper to align with the step **1** crease.

**3**

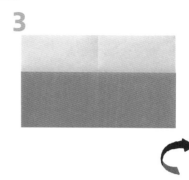

Turn the paper over.

**4**

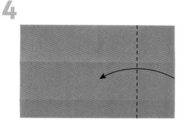

Fold the right edge to the center.

**5**

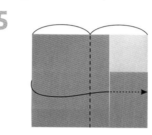

Fold in half, and tuck the left edge of the paper into the pocket.

**6**

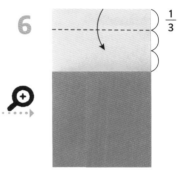

$\frac{1}{3}$

Fold along the dashed line.

**7**

Fold up the corners of the flap.

**8**

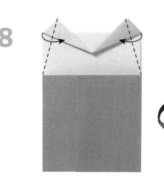

Fold along the dashed lines, and turn the paper over.

*Finished!*

Draw on the face.

Insert gum into the pocket.

# Pumpkin & Cat Pocket Pals

Photo on page 93

It can be used as a Halloween decoration or a treat holder!

## Main body

Start with the Kite Base (page 16).

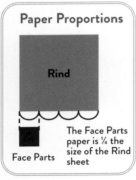

**Paper Proportions**

Rind

Face Parts

The Face Parts paper is ¼ the size of the Rind sheet

**1**

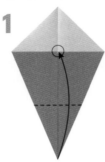

Fold the corner to meet the circled location.

**2**

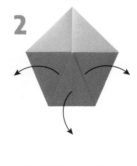

Unfold everything.

**3**

Make a step fold so that the corner sticks out slightly.

**4**

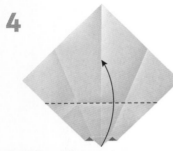

Fold along the existing crease.

**5**

Turn the paper over.

**6**

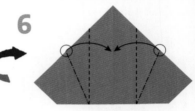

Grasp the circled locations, pull only the top layer to the center, and fold.

**7**

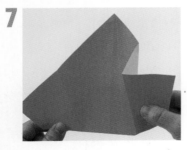

Step **6** in progress.

**8**

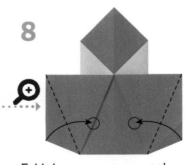

Fold the corners to meet the circled locations.

**9**

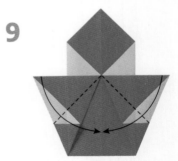

Fold the edges of the paper to align with the center.

**10**

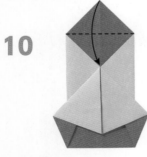

Fold along the dashed line.

**11**

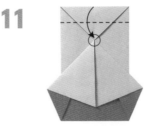

Fold the top edge of the paper to meet the circled location.

**12**

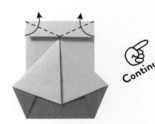

Continues

Fold up the corners of the flap.

98

**13**

Fold along the dashed lines.

**14**

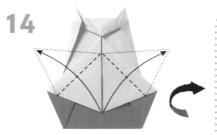

Fold the uppermost flaps diagonally so that the corners stick out, and turn it over.

Finished!

Draw a cat face and attach the Pumpkin Face Parts.

## Pumpkin Face Parts

Start by folding corner to corner both ways to install creases.

**1**

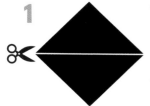

Cut in half.

**2**

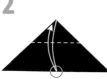

Fold the corner to meet the edge. Crease and unfold.

**3**

Cut along the step-**2** crease.

**4**

Cut as indicated, reserving one of the small squares.

**5**

The Pumpkin Face Parts are completed.

## Pumpkin & Bat Pocket Pals

Start by folding through step **13** of the Pumpkin & Cat Pocket Pals (begin with the colored side facing up).

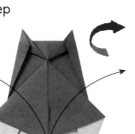

Unfold the flaps folded in step **9**, and turn the paper over.

Finished!

Draw a bat face and attach the Pumpkin Face Parts.

You can put treats inside.

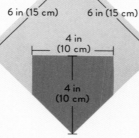

When you don't have double-sided origami paper...

If you want the Cat or Bat and the Pumpkin to have different colors (instead of one of them being white), you can simulate double-sided paper by gluing origami papers together, as shown to the right.

6 in (15 cm)   6 in (15 cm)

4 in (10 cm)

4 in (10 cm)

Turn the black paper over and glue the orange paper on top. Use the edge of the black paper as a guide for trimming.

**Tag (page 121)**
6 × 6 in (15 × 15 cm)

A mini wreath perfect for Halloween decorations. The atmosphere is created with black and orange.

**Life Ring Wreath (page 69)**
6 × 6 in (15 × 15 cm), 4 pieces

**Pumpkin & Cat Pocket Pals**
6 × 6 in (15 × 15 cm)

# Cat & Ghost Pocket Pals

Photo on page 93

Ghosts and cats are essential items for Halloween!

## Ghost

Start by folding through step **2** of the Pumpkin & Cat Pocket Pals (page 98).

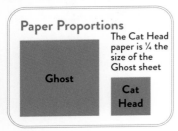

**Paper Proportions**

Ghost

The Cat Head paper is ¼ the size of the Ghost sheet

Cat Head

*The Cat Head is on page 27*

**1**

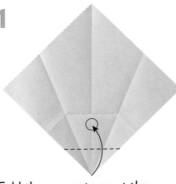

Fold the corner to meet the circled location.

**2**

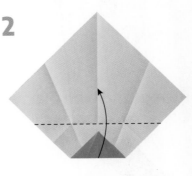

Fold along the existing crease.

**3**

Turn the paper over.

**4**

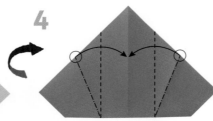

Grasp the circled locations, pull only the top layer to the center, and fold.

**5**

Step 4 in progress.

**6**

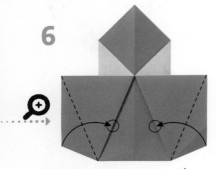

Fold the corners to meet the circled locations.

**7**

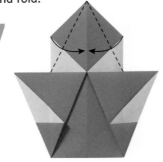

Fold along the dashed lines.

**8**

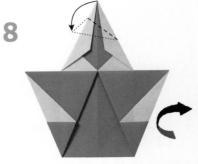

Fold diagonally so that the corner sticks out slightly, and turn it over.

**9**

The Ghost is completed. Draw on the face.

*Finished!*

Make and attach the Cat Head (page 27).

100

 Glue on your favorite creatures to decorate it sweetly.

**1**

¾ in (2 cm)

Fold the upper right edge to about ¾ in (2 cm) from the lower left edge. Unfold.

**2**

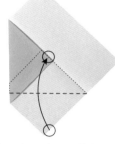

Fold the corner to align with the crease.

**3**

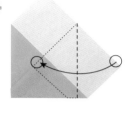

Align the edges of the paper (circled position to circled position).

**4**

Align the edges of the paper (circled position to circled position).

**5**

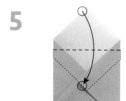

Align the edges of the paper (circled position to circled position).

**6**

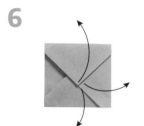

Open the three flaps.

**7**

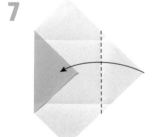

Fold along the existing crease.

**8**

Glue

Apply glue to the edge and fold along the existing crease.

**9**

Fold along the existing crease.

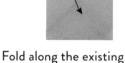 Finished!

### Square Envelope (page 92) size chart

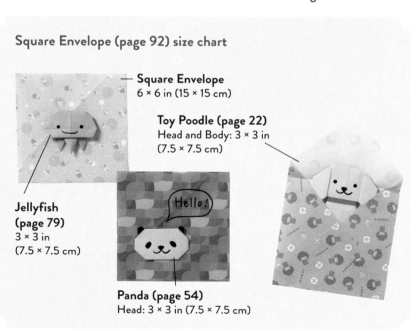

**Square Envelope**
6 × 6 in (15 × 15 cm)

**Toy Poodle (page 22)**
Head and Body: 3 × 3 in (7.5 × 7.5 cm)

**Jellyfish (page 79)**
3 × 3 in (7.5 × 7.5 cm)

Hello!

**Panda (page 54)**
Head: 3 × 3 in (7.5 × 7.5 cm)

# Animal Accessories

These cute and useful accessories can be used for everyday life and for special occasions. The stacked cat boxes also make fun decorations!

## Cute Small Animal Items

Instructions on page 105

**Panda Box**

Instructions on page 110

**Kitty Container**

Instructions on page 109

# Panda Chopstick Holder

Photo on page 102

With one more fold, you can turn me into a note card!

## Body

Start by folding the paper corner to corner and edge to edge both ways to install creases.

**1**

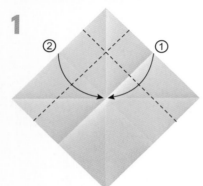

Fold the edges of the paper to meet the diagonal creases in the order of steps ①, then ②.

**2**

Fold the corner to the back and unfold to install a crease.

**3**

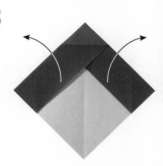

Open everything up.

**4**

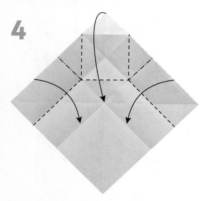

Use the creases to collapse the paper.

**5**

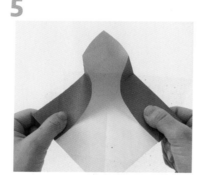

Step 4 in progress.

**6**

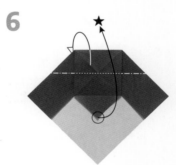

Fold the underlying layers along the dashed lines to the back, pivoting the corner marked ○ to the position marked ★.

**7**

Turn the paper over.

**8**

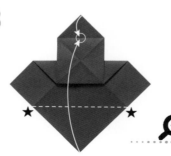

Fold the corners to the point marked ○. Fold the small underlying flaps at ★ up as well.

**9**

Continues

Tuck the triangular flaps inside.

## 10

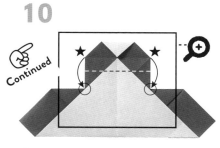

Fold the corners marked ★ to the points marked ○. Steps **11–12** show detail views.

## 11

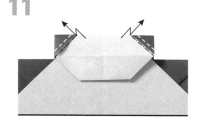

Step fold to the back along the dashed lines.

## 12

Fold small portions of the corners to the back.

## 13

Fold to the back along the dashed line.

*Finished!*

Draw on the face.

Fold the right side in mirror image at step **13** to make me a note card

Thank You

---

### Cute Animal Accessories (page 102) size chart

**Animal Bookmark (page 106)**
6 × 6 in (15 × 15 cm)

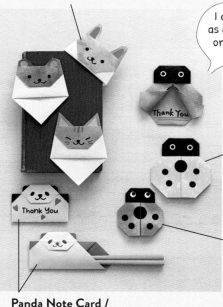

I can be used as a decoration or a message card!

**Ladybug Card (large) (page 108)**
Body: 6 × 6 in (15 × 15 cm)
Head: 3 × 3 in (7.5 × 7.5 cm)

**Ladybug Card (small)**
Body: 4¾ × 4¾ in (12 × 12 cm)
Head: 2 × 2 in (5 × 5 cm)

**Panda Note Card / Panda Chopstick Holder**
6 × 6 in (15 × 15 cm)

From *Kamikey's Seasonal Origami* (ISBN: 9784537216417):
**Cat Bookmark (page 50)**

There are plenty of cute and useful animal accessories in other Kamikey books too!

From *Kamikey's Kawaii Seasonal Origami* (ISBN: 9784537218282):
**Butterfly Envelope (page 54)**

From *Kamikey's Heartfelt Gift Origami* (ISBN: 9784537219517):

**Panda Envelope (page 53)**

**Heart & Cat Pocket (page 130)**

**Carp Streamer Chopstick Holder (page 83)**

# Animal Bookmarks

Photo on page 102

We make reading books even more fun!

## Cat

Start by folding corner to corner both ways to install creases.

**1**

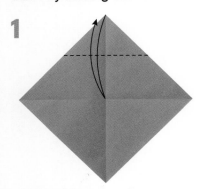

Fold the top corner to the center and unfold.

**2**

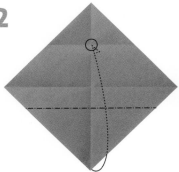

Fold the bottom corner behind to the indicated step-**1** crease intersection.

**3**

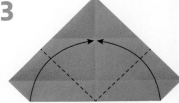

Align the bottom corners to the center and fold.

**4**

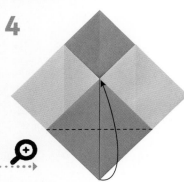

Fold the bottom corner up along the dashed line, allowing the underlying flap to swing out from behind.

**5**

Turn it over.

**6**

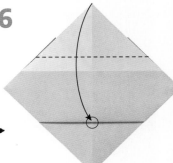

Align the top corner to the circled location and fold.

**7**

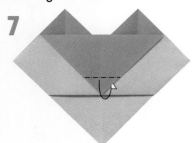

Fold backward along the dashed line, tucking the flap inside.

Insert the corner of a page into the bookmark's pocket

**8**

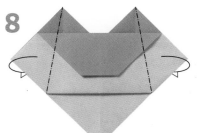

Fold backward along the dashed lines.

Finished!

Draw on the face.

106

## Bear

Start from a complete Cat Bookmark model.

Fold small portions of the corners behind.

Draw on the face.

## Rabbit

Begin by folding through step **3** of the Cat Bookmark.

**1**

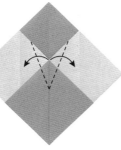

Fold the uppermost flaps along the dashed lines.

**2**

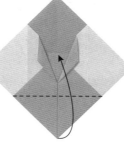

Fold the bottom corner up along the dashed line, allowing the underlying flap to swing out from behind.

**3**

Turn the paper over.

**4**

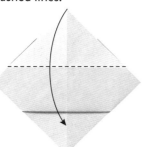

Fold the top corner down along the existing crease.

**5**

Fold the tip of the flap inside along the dashed line.

**6**

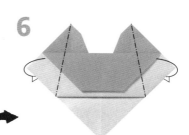

Fold backward along the dashed lines.

**7**

Fold small portions of the corners behind.

Draw on the face.

107

# Ladybug Card
Photo on page 102

Write a message and attach it to a wrapped gift; it's so cute!

## Head
Start by folding corner to corner both ways to install creases.

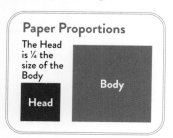

**Paper Proportions**

The Head is ¼ the size of the Body

Head

Body

**1** Fold the corners to the center.

**2** Fold in half.

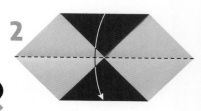

**3** Fold backward along the dashed lines.

**4** Fold the corners backward.

**5** The Head is completed.

## Body
Start by folding vertically in half to install a crease.

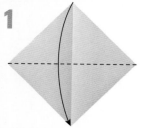

**1** Fold in half.

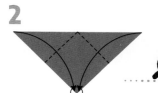

**2** Align the left and right corners to the circled corner and fold.

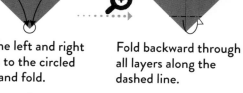

**3** Fold backward through all layers along the dashed line.

**4** Bring the outermost flaps back to the front.

**5** Inside reverse fold both flaps.

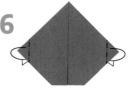

**6** Fold the corners behind.

**7** The Body is completed.

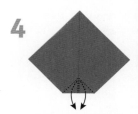

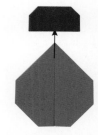

Insert the Body into the pocket of the Head and attach with glue.

Lift the wings and write a message.

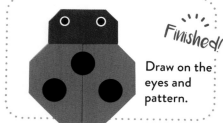

*Finished!*

Draw on the eyes and pattern.

108

# Kitty Container

Photo on page 103

This is a cute cat-faced box with upright ears

Start from the Blintz Base (Page 16).

**1**

Fold the edges to the middle, unfolding after each.

**2**

Open the top and bottom flaps.

**3**

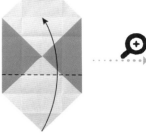

Fold along the existing crease.

**4**

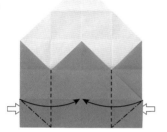

Open pockets at the ⇨ ⇦ symbols and flatten the corners into triangles.

**5**

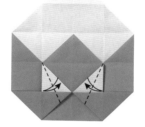

Fold the flaps to bisect the angles. Unfold.

**6**

Fold the flaps to bisect the angles.

**7**

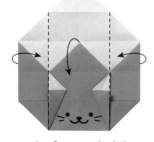

Draw on the face, and while raising the face panel upright, also lift the sides to make them three-dimensional.

**8**

Fold along the existing creases, tucking the paper in so it aligns with the inner walls.

**9**

Raise the corners and fold along the dashed lines to make the back three-dimensional.

**10**

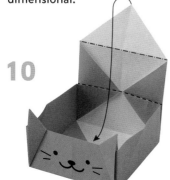

Fold along the dashed lines and tuck the paper in so it aligns with the inner walls.

Finished!

It's fun to put in some snacks to share, or line boxes up to decorate!

Start from the Blintz Base (Page 16).

**1**

Fold the edges to the middle, unfolding after each.

**2**

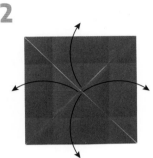

Unfold entirely.

**3**

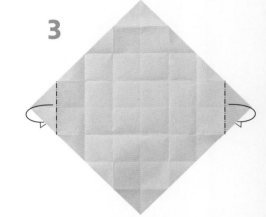

Fold backward along the existing creases.

**4**

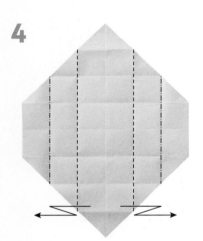

Leave the folds from step **3** in place, and make step folds along the existing creases.

**5**

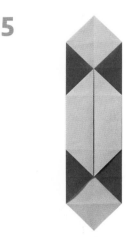

Turn it over.

**6**

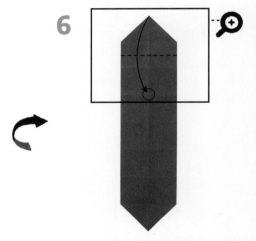

Align the top corner to the circled location and fold. Steps **7–9** show detail views.

**7**

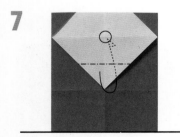

Align the corner to the circled location and fold inside along the dashed line.

**8**

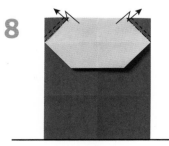

Step fold to the back along the dashed lines.

**9**

Fold small portions of the corners behind.

Continues

**10**

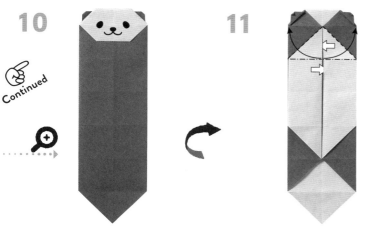

Continued

Draw on the face and turn it over.

**11**

Open the pockets from the ⇨ ⇦ symbols and make the paper three-dimensional.

**12**

Apply glue.

Apply glue and adhere the layers of the front of the box together.

**13**

Fold the flaps to the outside.

**14**

Step **13** completed. Rotate the box and view it from above.

**15**

Raise the corners and fold along the dashed lines to make the back three-dimensional.

**16**

Step **15** in progress.

**17**

Fold along the dashed lines and tuck the paper in so it aligns with the inner walls.

Finished!

# Projects for January to June

I've created twelve months of animal decorations using the items introduced so far. Decorate your home or entryway according to the seasons and events.

## January

**Flower (page 117)**
Large: 3 × 3 in (7.5 × 7.5 cm)
Small: 2 × 2 in (5 × 5 cm)

**Frame (page 142)**
6 × 6 in (15 × 15 cm)

**Leaf (page 57)**
1½ × 3 in
(3.75 × 7.5 cm)

**Papier-Mâché Dog (page 114)**
Head: 6 × 6 in (15 × 15 cm)
Body: 6 × 6 in (15 × 15 cm)
Scarf: 3 × 3 in (7.5 × 7.5 cm)

**Sea Bream (page 116)**
4¾ × 4¾ in (12 × 12 cm)

## February

**Tag (page 121)**
6 × 6 in (15 × 15 cm)

**Heart Wreath (page 118)**
6 × 6 in (15 × 15 cm)

**Heart Rabbit (page 120)**
6 × 6 in (15 × 15 cm)

LOVE

## March

**Leaf (page 43)**
2 × 2 in (5 × 5 cm)

**Rabbit Hina Dolls (page 124)**
Obina & Mebina: 6 × 6 in (15 × 15 cm)
Scepter: 1½ × 3 in (3.75 × 7.5 cm)
Fan (small parts): 2 × 2 in (5 × 5 cm)

**Fan (page 122)**
Large parts: 6 × 6 in
(15 × 15 cm)
Small parts: 3 × 3 in
(7.5 × 7.5 cm)

**Cherry Blossoms (page 117)**
3 × 3 in (7.5 × 7.5 cm)

## April

**Butterfly Wreath (page 51)**
3 × 6 in (7.5 × 15 cm)

**Ladybug Boy (page 88)**
Head & Body: 4¾ × 4¾ in (12 × 12 cm)

**Bumblebee Boy (page 90)**
Head & Body: 4¾ × 4¾ in (12 × 12 cm)
Wings: 2 × 2 in (5 × 5 cm)

**Tag (page 121)**
6 × 6 in (15 × 15 cm)

Be Healthy

## May

**Axe (page 127)**
3 × ¾ in
(7.5 × 2 cm)

**Carp Streamer (page 128)**
Carp: 3 × 3 in (7.5 × 7.5 cm)
Streamer: 3 × 1½ in (7.5 × 3.75 cm)
Pole: 6 × 1½ in (15 × 3.75 cm)
Pinwheel: 3 × 3 in (7.5 × 7.5 cm)

**Kintaro (page 126)**
Main body: 6 × 6 in
(15 × 15 cm)
Apron: 1½ × 1½ in
(3.75 × 3.75 cm)

## June

**Frog Toothpick Holder (page 96)**
4¾ × 4¾ in (12 × 12 cm)

**Simple Wreath (page 141)**
6 × 6 in (15 × 15 cm)

**Bear (page 127)**
Head & Body: 3 × 6 in (7.5 × 15 cm)
Muzzle: 1½ × 1½ in (3.75 × 3.75 cm)

**Snail (page 44)**
Large: 6 × 6 in (15 × 15 cm)
Small: 3 × 3 in (7.5 × 7.5 cm)

**Hydrangea (page 42)**
6 × 6 in (15 × 15 cm)

**Leaf (page 43)**
3 × 3 in (7.5 × 7.5 cm)

**Frame (page 142)**
6 × 6 in (15 × 15 cm)

# Papier-mâché Dog

Photo on page 112

Decorate for the New Year with an auspicious papier-mâché puppy figurine!

## Head

Start by folding corner to corner both ways to install creases.

**Paper Proportions**

Head

Body

Body 1/4 Size

Scarf

**1** Align the top corner to the center and fold.

**2** Fold the bottom corner to the top edge.

**3** Fold in small portions of the bottom corners.

**4** Align the edges of the paper to the center crease line.

**5** Fold along the dashed line. Turn the paper over.

**6** Fold along the dashed lines to install creases, and unfold.

**7** Inside reverse fold along the existing creases.

**8** Fold the corners of the top layer inside.

**9** Fold backward along the dashed lines.

**10** The Head is completed. Draw on the face.

## Bib

Start by folding in half to install a vertical crease.

**1**

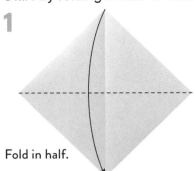

Fold in half.

**2**

Fold backward through all layers along the dashed line.

**3**

The Bib is completed.

## Body

Start by folding through step **1** of the Bib.

**1**

Fold the bottom corner of the uppermost layer to the top edge. Unfold.

**2**

Align the step **1** crease with the top edge and make a pinch mark only along the dashed part.

**3**

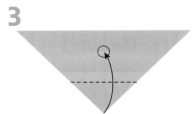

Fold both layers of the bottom corner to the indicated step **2** pinch mark.

**4**

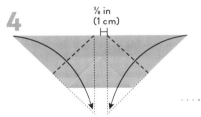

Fold down flaps about ⅜ in (1 cm) offset from the center crease.

**5**

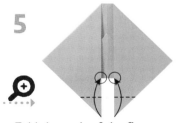

Fold the ends of the flaps up to meet the circled locations.

**6**

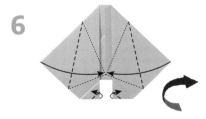

Fold the outside corners in, and turn the paper over.

**7**

The Body is completed.

## Assembly Instructions

**1**

Place the Bib on the Body and fold the outside corners behind, gluing it in place.

**2**

Attach the Head.

Finished!

115

# Sea Bream

Photo on page 112

Photo on page 112

> Besides a wreath, it would also look nice on New Year's cards and other items.

Start from the Fish Base (Page 16).

## 1

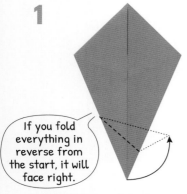

> If you fold everything in reverse from the start, it will face right.

Fold all layers of the bottom corner diagonally.

## 2

Fold to bisect the angle on the top flap only.

## 3

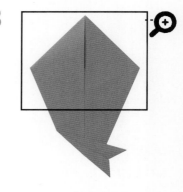

Step 2 completed. Steps 4–6 show detail views.

## 4

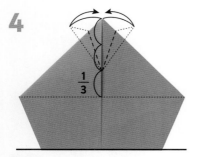

1/3

Fold along the dashed lines to install creases. Unfold.

## 5

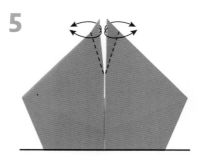

Outside reverse fold along the existing creases.

## 6

Fold over the projecting ends of the flaps. Rotate the paper.

## 7

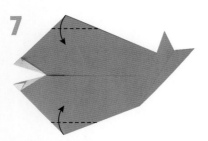

Fold in the corners.

## 8

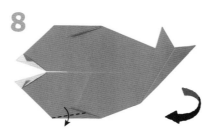

Fold diagonally so the corner is visible below the bottom edge. Flip the paper over top to bottom.

Finished!

Draw on the eyes, fins and gill.

# Flower Cutouts
Photo on page 112

You can create stars and flower shapes with five petals.

## Basic Pentagon Shape

**1**

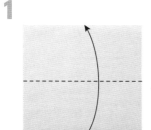

Fold in half.

**2**

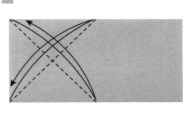

Fold the left corners diagonally as shown. Unfold after each.

**3**

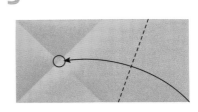

Align the corner to the circled location and fold.

**4**

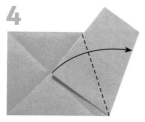

Align the corner of the uppermost flap with the outside edge of the paper.

**5**

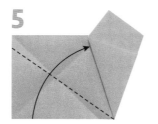

Align the bottom edge of the paper with the folded edge of the uppermost flap.

**6**

Fold backward along the dashed line.

**7**

The Basic Pentagon Shape is completed.

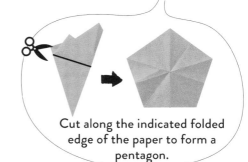

Cut along the indicated folded edge of the paper to form a pentagon.

## Cutting Instructions

**1**

Flower    Cherry Blossom    Star    Starfish

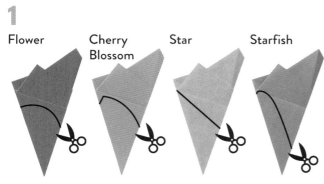

Cut along the bold lines.

**2**

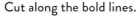

Open everything up.

Cherry Blossom

Flower

Star

Starfish

Finished!

# Heart Wreath

Photo on page 112

## Parts

Prepare 8 pieces of paper of the same size, and start by folding them in half to install vertical and diagonal creases.

**1**

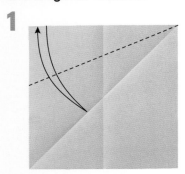

Fold the top edge to the diagonal crease. Unfold.

**2**

Align the top left corner to the circled location and fold horizontally.

**3**

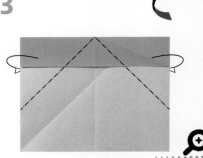

Fold the top corners behind to the center. Turn the paper over.

**4**

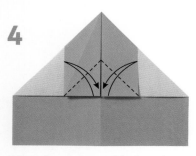

Align the corners with the edges of the paper. Crease and unfold.

**5**

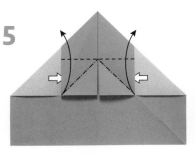

Open pockets at the ⇨ ⇦ symbols and flatten them.

**6**

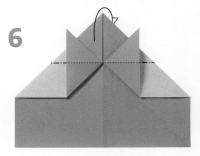

Fold the underlying flap backward along the dashed line.

**7**

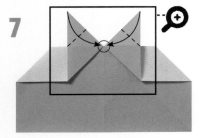

Fold the corners as indicated. Step **8** shows a detail view.

**8**

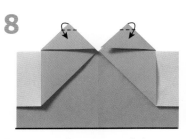

Fold in small portions of the corners.

**9**

Fold the bottom edge of the paper to the circled location. Turn the paper over.

**10**

Fold the top corners along the dashed lines and tuck them inside.

**11**

Make 8 of these.

In the instructions, we made 4 pieces each in 2 colors, but make them in any color or combination you like!

# Assembly Instructions

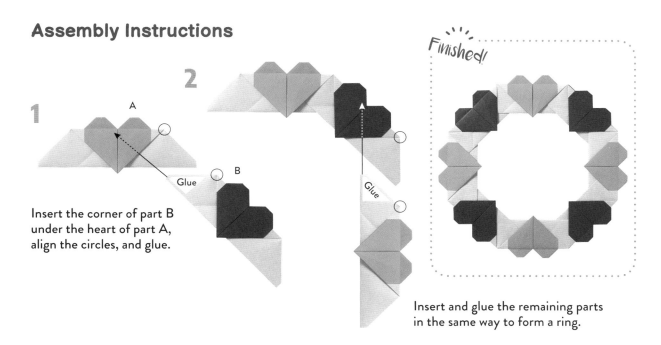

**1** A

Insert the corner of part B under the heart of part A, align the circles, and glue.

Glue

B

**2** Glue

**Finished!**

Insert and glue the remaining parts in the same way to form a ring.

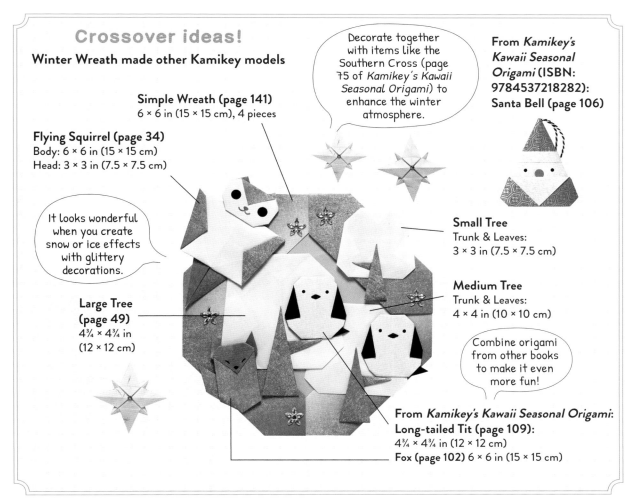

## Crossover ideas!

**Winter Wreath made other Kamikey models**

Decorate together with items like the Southern Cross (page 75 of *Kamikey's Kawaii Seasonal Origami*) to enhance the winter atmosphere.

From *Kamikey's Kawaii Seasonal Origami* (ISBN: 9784537218282): Santa Bell (page 106)

**Simple Wreath (page 141)**
6 × 6 in (15 × 15 cm), 4 pieces

**Flying Squirrel (page 34)**
Body: 6 × 6 in (15 × 15 cm)
Head: 3 × 3 in (7.5 × 7.5 cm)

It looks wonderful when you create snow or ice effects with glittery decorations.

**Large Tree (page 49)**
4¾ × 4¾ in (12 × 12 cm)

**Small Tree**
Trunk & Leaves:
3 × 3 in (7.5 × 7.5 cm)

**Medium Tree**
Trunk & Leaves:
4 × 4 in (10 × 10 cm)

Combine origami from other books to make it even more fun!

From *Kamikey's Kawaii Seasonal Origami*:
**Long-tailed Tit (page 109):**
4¾ × 4¾ in (12 × 12 cm)
**Fox (page 102)** 6 × 6 in (15 × 15 cm)

Fold a heart with a cute rabbit from a single sheet.

Start by folding edge to edge both ways to install creases.

**1**

Fold to the center.

**2**

Fold to the center.

**3**

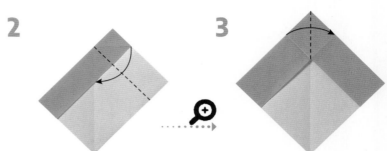

Fold the top corner along the dashed line.

**4**

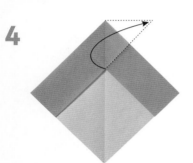

Grasp and pull out the top corner, then fold it to the right.

**5**

Pull out the part you are holding.

**6**

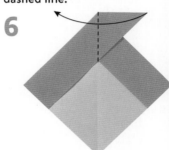

Fold along the dashed line to the left.

**7**

Open the pocket at the ⇨ symbol and flatten it.

**8**

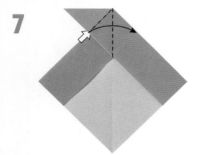

Fold backward along the dashed line.

**9**

Open pockets at the ⇦⇨ symbols and flatten them.

**10**

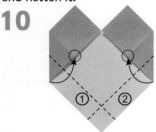

Fold the corners to meet the circled locations, first ①, then ②.

**11**

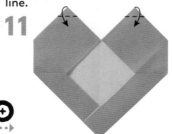

Fold in the corners, and then turn the paper over.

**12**

Continues

Fold a small portion of the indicated corner.

120

Write a message, stick it on a present, or use it as a wreath decoration.

Start from the Pig Base (page 17).

## 1

Fold corner to corner in four location.

## 2

Fold the top and bottom edges to the center.

## 3

Turn the paper over.

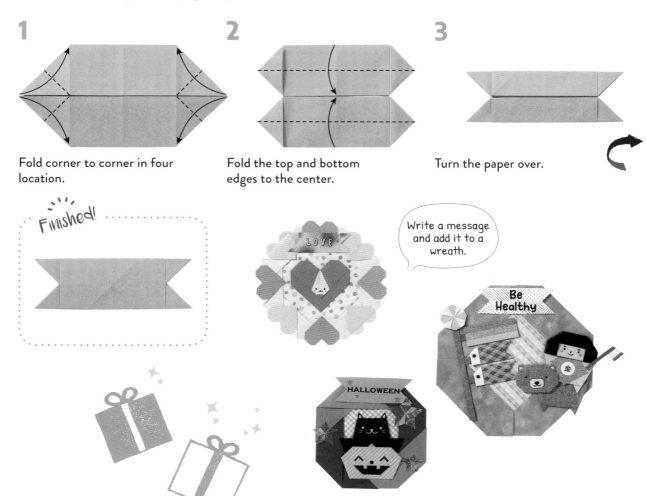

Finished!

Write a message and add it to a wreath.

## 13

Fold the top layer along the dashed line.

Continued

## 14

Fold inside along the dashed lines.

Finished!

Draw on the face.

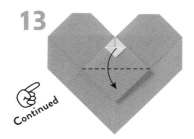

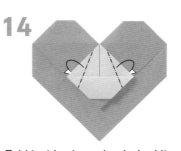

Make with pretty paper, and it can be used as a decoration as it is, or as a base for a wreath.

## Small Part

Start by folding in half to install a vertical crease.

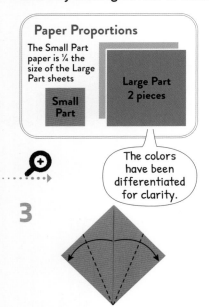

### Paper Proportions

The Small Part paper is ¼ the size of the Large Part sheets

Small Part

Large Part 2 pieces

The colors have been differentiated for clarity.

**1**

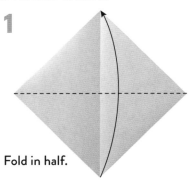

Fold in half.

**2**

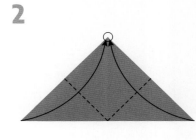

Fold the left and right corners to the center.

**3**

Fold the inside edges to meet the outside edges.

**4**

Fold backward along the dashed lines.

**5**

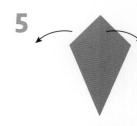

Return to the state of step **2**.

**6**

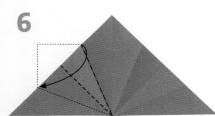

Grasp the mountain crease and fold the section using the existing creases, shifting the paper.

**7**

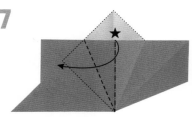

Fold over the ★ crease as a mountain fold, and shift the top layer along the existing creases as in step **6**.

**8**

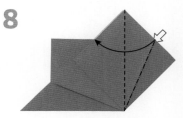

Open the a pocket at the ⤸ symbol and flatten it.

**9**

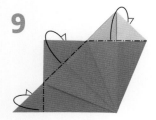

Fold backward along the dashed lines.

**10**

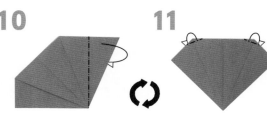

Fold backward along the dashed line. Rotate the paper.

**11**

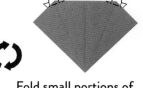

Fold small portions of the corners backward.

**12**

The Small Part is completed.

# Large Part

**1**

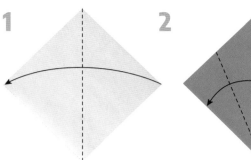

Fold in half.

**2**

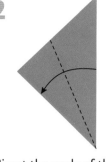

Bisect the angle of the paper and fold.

**3**

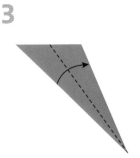

Bisect the angle and fold the top flap only.

**4**

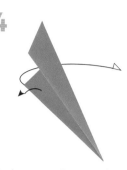

Open everything and display the colored side.

**5**

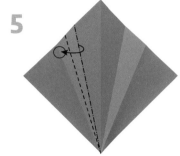

Grasp the mountain crease and fold the section using the existing creases, shifting the paper.

**6**

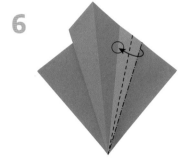

Grasp the mountain crease and fold it to meet the circled crease.

**7**

The Large Part is completed. Make two of these.

# Assembly

**1**

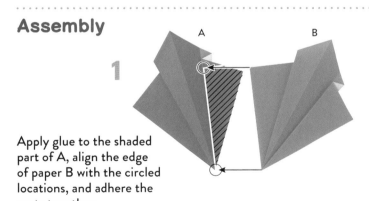

Apply glue to the shaded part of A, align the edge of paper B with the circled locations, and adhere the parts together.

**2**

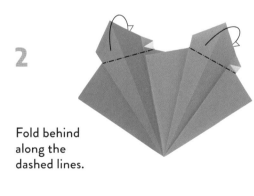

Fold behind along the dashed lines.

Finished!

**3**

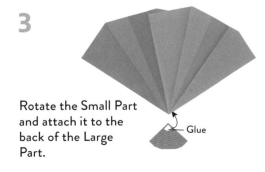

Rotate the Small Part and attach it to the back of the Large Part.

Glue

123

# Rabbit Hina Dolls

Photo on page 112

The rounded form makes for a cute Rabbit Hina Doll.

## Scepter (Shaku)

Start with the Kite Base (page 16).

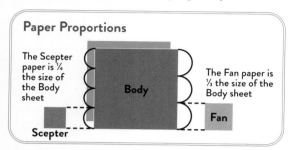

**Paper Proportions**

The Scepter paper is ¼ the size of the Body sheet

Body

The Fan paper is ⅓ the size of the Body sheet

Scepter

Fan

*The Fan held by Ohina-sama is the same as the Small Part on page 122*

**1**

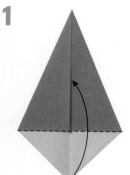

Fold along the dashed line.

**2**

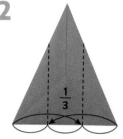

⅓

Fold along the dashed lines, overlapping the corners.

**3**

Fold in the corner, and turn the paper over.

**4**

The Scepter is completed.

## Crossover ideas!

**Hinamatsuri Wreath made using Kamikey's other books**

Combine with other origami from different books for more fun!

From *Kamikey's Kawaii Seasonal Origami* (ISBN: 9784537218282) (the same applies to the other ★ items): March Wreath (page 120)

Leaf (this book, page 43) 2 × 2 in (5 × 5 cm)

From the ★ book: Yaezakura (page 50) 3 × 3 in (7.5 × 7.5 cm)

From *Kamikey's Seasonal Origami* (ISBN: 9784537216417) Bonbori (page 28) Lantern: 4¾ × 2 in (12 × 6 cm) Stand: 4 × 2 in (10 × 5 cm)

From the ★ book: Full Moon Rabbit, Large (page 86) (Odairi-sama and Ohina-sama) 6 × 6 in (15 × 15 cm)

Full Moon Rabbit, Small (Sannin Kanjo) 4¾ × 4¾ in (12 × 12 cm)

It's a wreath with Nekobina and Hishimochi.

The tools held by the Hina dolls are made by cutting paper.

**Simple Wreath (this book, page 141)** 6 × 6 in (15 × 15 cm)

# Body

Start with the Square Base (page 15) (rotated so the open side is facing up).

**1**

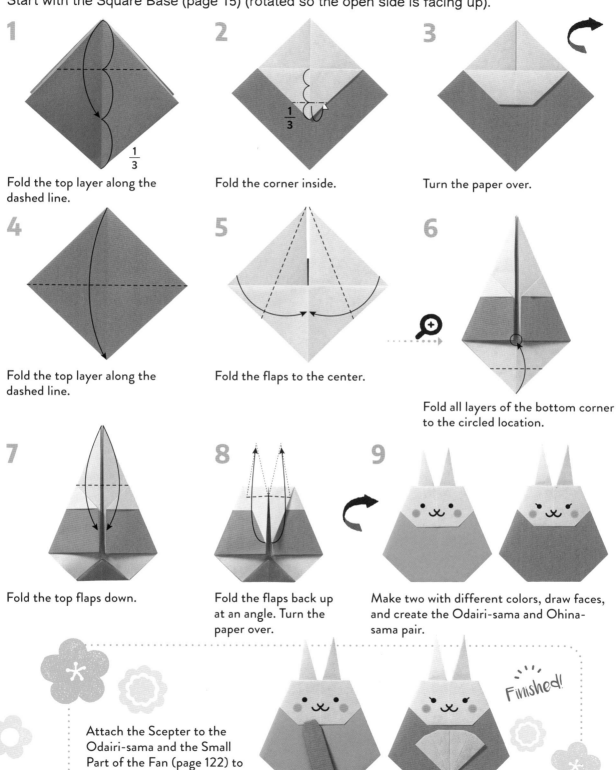

$\frac{1}{3}$

Fold the top layer along the dashed line.

**2**

$\frac{1}{3}$

Fold the corner inside.

**3**

Turn the paper over.

**4**

Fold the top layer along the dashed line.

**5**

Fold the flaps to the center.

**6**

Fold all layers of the bottom corner to the circled location.

**7**

Fold the top flaps down.

**8**

Fold the flaps back up at an angle. Turn the paper over.

**9**

Make two with different colors, draw faces, and create the Odairi-sama and Ohina-sama pair.

Attach the Scepter to the Odairi-sama and the Small Part of the Fan (page 122) to the Ohina-sama.

Finished!

It would be nice to decorate with the carp streamers too, for Children's Day.

## Kintaro

Start by folding in half to install a vertical crease.

**1**

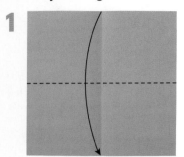

Fold in half.

**2**

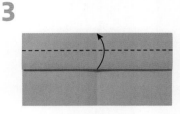

Fold the top layer in half.

**3**

Fold the top flap in half.

**4**

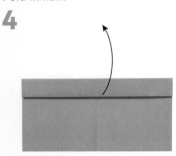

Unfold everything.

**5**

Fold along the crease.

**6**

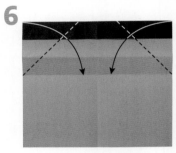

Fold the corners to align with the horizontal crease.

**7**

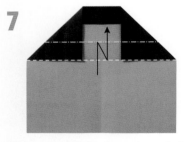

Make a step fold along the existing creases.

**8**

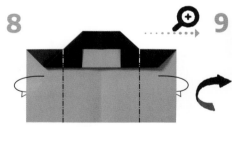

Fold backward along the dashed lines, and turn it over.

**9**

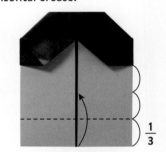

Fold along the dashed line.

$\frac{1}{3}$

**10**

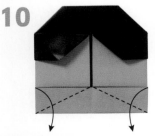

Fold the corners of the flap along the dashed lines.

**11**

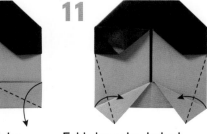

Fold along the dashed lines, and turn it over.

**12**

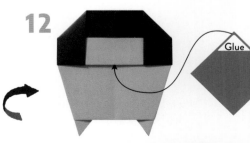

Glue

Prepare the Apron paper (1½ × 1½ in / 3.75 × 3.75 cm), insert it, and attach it with glue.

Continues

## Paper Proportions

Cut a full sheet in half.

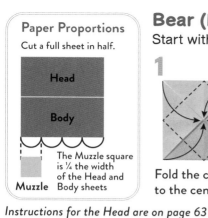

The Muzzle square is ¼ the width of the Head and Body sheets

*Instructions for the Head are on page 63*

# Bear (Muzzle)

Start with the Blintz Base (page 16).

**1**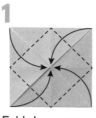

Fold the corners to the center.

**2**

Fold the top and bottom corners to the center. Fold in a small portion of the side corners, and turn the paper over.

**3**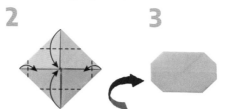

The Muzzle is completed.

Make the Head of the Tiger (page 63), attach the Muzzle and draw on the face.

## Body

Start from the Body of the Chihuahua (page 24).

**1**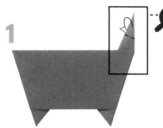

Fold backward along the dashed line. Step **2** is a detail view.

**2**

Fold a small portion of the corner backward.

**3**

The Body is completed.

*Finished!*

Attach the Head to the Body.

## Axe

Begin with a central horizontal crease.

### Paper Proportions

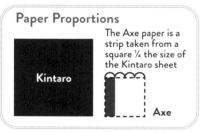

The Axe paper is a strip taken from a square ¼ the size of the Kintaro sheet

*The proportions above are applicable when appearing with the Kintaro model*

*Finished!*

👉 **Continued**

Draw on the face.

**1**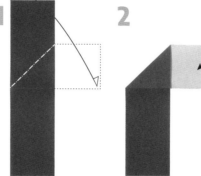

Fold backward along the dashed line.

**2**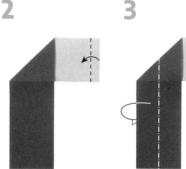

Fold along the dashed line.

**3**

Fold the blue part in half to the back.

**4**

Fold the blue part in half to the back.

**5**

Fold backward along the dashed line.

*Finished!*

# Carp and Streamers

Photo on page 113

It's a cute miniature carp streamer.

## Carp

Start by folding edge to edge both ways to install creases.

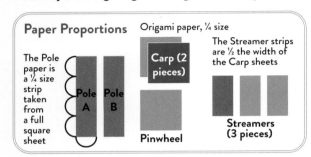

**Paper Proportions**

Origami paper, ¼ size

The Pole paper is a ¼ size strip taken from a full square sheet

Pole A | Pole B

Carp (2 pieces)

Pinwheel

The Streamer strips are ½ the width of the Carp sheets

Streamers (3 pieces)

**1**

$\frac{1}{3}$

Fold backward along the dashed line.

**2**

Fold to the center.

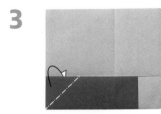

**3**

Fold the flap's left corner inside, aligning it with the hidden crease.

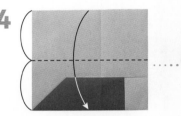

**4**

Fold in half, top to bottom.

**5**

Fold the corner of the top layer inside, aligning it with the hidden crease.

**6**

Cut along the bold line.

**7**

Fold the flaps along the dashed lines, tuck them inside, and then turn the paper over.

**8**

Fold backward along the dashed line.

**9**

The Carp is completed. Make two in different colors. Draw on eyes.

### Crossover ideas!

**Mother's Day and Father's Day cards made using another book**

**From *Kamikey's Heartfelt Gift Origami*** (ISBN: 9784537219517):

Heart (page 131) 6 × 6 in (15 × 15 cm)

Combine with other origami from different books for more fun!

I love you, Mom

Thank you, Dad

Panda (this book, page 54)
Head: 3 × 3 in (7.5 × 7.5 cm)

# Pinwheel

Start from the Blintz Base (page 16).

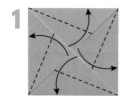

**1** Fold out each corner, aligning them with the edges of the paper.

**2** Turn the paper over.

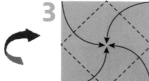

**3** Fold only the top layer corners to the center.

**4** Fold backward along the dashed lines.

**5** Fold the corners to the back.

**6** The Pinwheel is completed.

Finished!

Attach the Pinwheel, Streamers, and Carp to the Pole.

# Pole

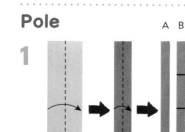

**1** Fold in half, then fold in half again. Make two of these and cut one along the bold lines.

**2** For A, lift the uppermost flap, and for B, position segments horizontally (use three pieces).

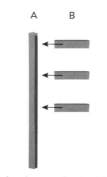

**3** Apply glue to the inside of A, insert B, and attach them together.

**4** The Pole is completed.

# Streamers

Start by folding in half to install a horizontal crease.

**1** Fold the top edge to the center. Make three of these.

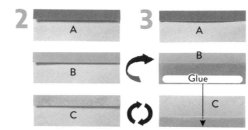

**2** Turn B over and rotate C 180 degrees.

**3** Apply glue and insert B under the flap of C, attaching them together.

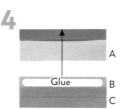

**4** Apply glue and insert B and C under the flap of A, attaching them together.

**5** The Streamers are completed.

# Projects for July to December

**Star (page 117)**
Large: 3 × 3 in (7.5 × 7.5 cm)
Small: 2 × 2 in (5 × 5 cm)

**July**

**Frame (page 142)**
6 × 6 in (15 × 15 cm)

**Bamboo (page 57)**
Branch: 6 × 1½ in (15 × 3.75 cm)
Leaf: 3 × 1½ in (7.5 × 3.75 cm)

**Simple Wreath (page 141)**
6 × 6 in (15 × 15 cm)

**Shell (page 80)**
3 × 3 in (7.5 × 7.5 cm)

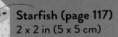
**August**

**Starfish (page 117)**
2 × 2 in (5 x 5 cm)

**Bicolor Fish (page 78)**
1½ × 3 in (3.75 × 7.5 cm)

**Dog Orihime and Hikoboshi (page 132)**
Orihime and Hikoboshi: 6 × 6 in (15 × 15 cm)
Scarf: 6 × 1½ in (15 × 3.75 cm)
Belt: ¼ × 4 in (7 mm × 10 cm)

**Wave (page 133)**
3 × 3 in (7.5 × 7.5 cm)

**September**

**Whale (page 72)**
Large: 6 × 6 in (15 × 15 cm)
Spout: 3 × 1½ in (7.5 × 3.75 cm)
Small: 4¾ × 4¾ in (12 × 12 cm)

**Simple Maple Leaf (page 46)**
3 × 3 in (7.5 × 7.5 cm)

**Cloud (page 136)**
3 × 3 in (7.5 × 7.5 cm)

**Simple Wreath (page 141)**
6 × 6 in (15 × 15 cm)

**Pestle (page 136)**
4¾ × 1 in (12 × 2.5 cm)

**Mochi-Pounding Rabbit (page 134)**
Head and Body: 6 × 6 in (15 × 15 cm)
Clothes: 3 × 3 in (7.5 × 7.5 cm)

**Mortar (page 136)**
4¾ × 1 in (12 × 5 cm)

**Life Ring Wreath (page 69)**
6 × 6 in (15 × 15 cm)

**Star (page 117)**
Large: 2 × 2 in (5 × 5 cm)
Medium: 1½ × 1½ in (3.75 × 3.75 cm)
Small: 1 × 1 in (2.5 × 2.5 cm)

**Pumpkin & Bat Pocket (page 99)**
6 × 6 in (15 × 15 cm)

**October**

**Cat Cosplay (page 86)**
Head: 3 × 3 in (7.5 × 7.5 cm)
Body: 6 × 6 in (15 × 15 cm)
Cat Ears: 3 × 3 in (7.5 × 7.5 cm)
Tail: ¾ × 3 in (2 × 7.5 cm)

**Cat (page 26)**
Head and Body: 3 × 3 in (7.5 × 7.5 cm)

**Dragonfly (page 47)**
Body: 3 × 3 in (7.5 × 7.5 cm)
Wings: 3 × 3 in (7.5 × 7.5 cm)

**Pumpkin & Cat Pocket (page 98)**
6 × 6 in (15 × 15 cm)

**Cat & Ghost Pocket (page 100)**
Ghost: 6 × 6 in (15 × 15 cm)
Cat Face: 3 × 3 in (7.5 × 7.5 cm)

**Simple Wreath (page 141)**
6 × 6 in (15 × 15 cm)

**November**

**Simple Wreath (page 141)**
6 × 6 in (15 × 15 cm)

**Leaf (page 43)**
1½ × 1½ in (3.75 × 3.75 cm)

**Owl (page 38)**
Body (Large): 6 × 6 in (15 × 15 cm)
Body (Small): 4¾ × 4¾ in (12 × 12 cm)
Eyes and Beak Parts
(Large): 3 × 3 in (7.5 × 7.5 cm)
(Small): 2 × 2 in (5 × 5 cm)

**Bagworm (page 48)**
3 × 3 in (7.5 × 7.5 cm)

**Tree (page 49)**
Trunk and Leaves:
6 × 6 in (15 × 15 cm)

**Tag (page 121)**
6 × 6 in (15 × 15 cm)

**Simple Wreath (page 141)**
6 × 6 in (15 × 15 cm)

**Tree (page 49)**
Trunk and Leaves:
3 × 3 in (7.5 × 7.5 cm)

**December**

**Santa Hat (page 137)**
3 × 3 in (7.5 × 7.5 cm)

**Polar Bear Pocket Pal (page 67)**
6 × 6 in (15 × 15 cm)

**Reindeer (page 138)**
Head and Body:
6 × 6 in (15 × 15 cm)
Nose: 1½ × 1½ in (3.75 × 3.75 cm)

merry christmas!

**Sled (page 140)**
Part A: 6 × 6 in (15 × 15 cm)
Part B: 3 × 6 in (7.5 × 15 cm)
Rope: 1½ × 6 in (3.75 × 15 cm)

It would be nice as a hanging decoration too!

## Orihime

Start from step **4** of the Rabbit Hina Dolls Body (page 125).

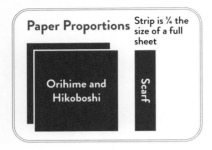

**Paper Proportions** Strip is ¼ the size of a full sheet

Orihime and Hikoboshi

Scarf

**1**

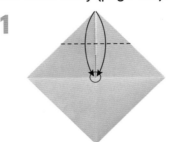

Fold the corners to meet the circled location.

**2**

Align the edges of the paper with the vertical crease.

**3**

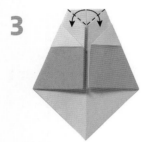

Fold along the dashed lines.

**4**

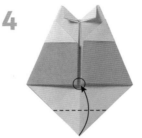

Fold the corner to the circled location, and turn it over.

**5**

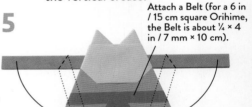

Attach a Belt (for a 6 in / 15 cm square Orihime, the Belt is about ¼ × 4 in / 7 mm × 10 cm).

Using the Scarf paper, make Pole A (page 129), place it under Orihime, and fold along the dashed lines.

**6**

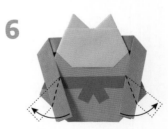

Fold along the dashed line.

Finished!

Draw on the faces. For Hikoboshi, fold through step **4** and attach the Belt.

---

### Crossover ideas!

**Summer Wreath made using another book**

**Simple Wreath (this book, page 141)**
6 × 6 in (15 × 15 cm), 4 pieces

Combine with other origami from different books for more fun!

**From Kamikey's Kawaii Seasonal Origami (ISBN: 9784537218282):**
**Dandelion (page 56)**
Flower: 4¾ × 4¾ in (12 × 12 cm)
Leaf: 3 × 3 in (7.5 × 7.5 cm), 2 pieces
Stem: 4¾ x 1 in (12 x 2.5 cm)

**Butterfly (this book, page 50)**
Body: 2 × 4 in (5 × 10 cm)
Antenna: 2 × ½ in (5 × 1.25 cm)

**Butterfly Girl (this book, page 91)**
Body: 6 × 6 in (15 × 15 cm)
Head: 3 × 3 in (7.5 × 7.5 cm)
Wings: 3 × 3 in (7.5 × 7.5 cm)
Antenna: about 3 × ¾ in (7.5 × 2 cm)

# Wave

Photo on page 130

Large, wavy lines are perfect for summer decorations.

## Parts

Prepare at least 2 pieces and start by folding in half vertically.

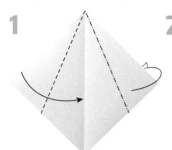

**1** Fold to the center from both the front and back.

**2** Fold along the dashed line, and tuck the left side under the triangular flap.

**3** Bring the right corner to the top. Make a pinch mark only where indicated.

**4** Align the top corner with the circled location. Crease and unfold.

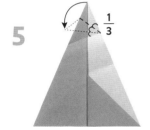

**5** Fold the corner at about a ⅓ angle.

**6** Fold along the existing crease.

**7** Fold backward along the dashed line.

**8** The Part is completed. Make two or more.

## Assembly

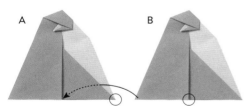

Insert corner B into pocket A, align the circles, and glue them together.

You can connect as many as you like!

Finished!

### Crossover ideas!

**Summer Wreath made using another book**

From *Kamikey's Heartfelt Gift Origami* (ISBN: 9784537219517):
**Constellation base (page 23)**
3 × 3 in (7.5 × 7.5 cm), 2 pieces

Combine with other origami from different books for more fun!

**Simple Wreath (this book, page 141)**
6 × 6 in (15 × 15 cm), 4 pieces

**Crab (small) (this book, page 81)**
4¾ × 4¾ in (12 × 12 cm)

**Crab (large)**
6 × 6 in (15 × 15 cm)

**Polar Bear (this book, page 66)**
6 × 6 in (15 × 15 cm)

**Penguin (this book, page 70)**
6 × 6 in (15 × 15 cm)

From *Kamikey's Seasonal Origami* (ISBN: 9784537216417)
**Watermelon (page 69)**
Flesh: 2 × 2 in (5 × 5 cm)
Rind: ½ × 2 in (1.25 × 5 cm)

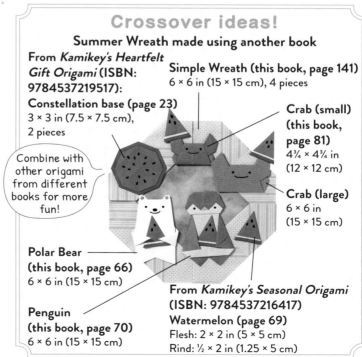

# Mochi Making Rabbit

Photo on page 130

Let's prepare the mortar and pestle and make them a part of the moon-viewing decoration.

## Rabbit (Head)

Start by folding in half vertically.

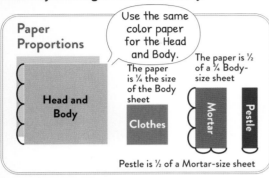

Paper Proportions

Use the same color paper for the Head and Body.

Head and Body

The paper is ¼ the size of the Body sheet

Clothes

The paper is ½ of a ¼ Body-size sheet

Mortar

Pestle

Pestle is ½ of a Mortar-size sheet

**1**

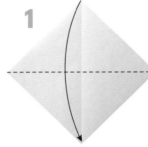

Fold in half.

**2**

1 in (2.5 cm)

Fold at 1 in (2.5 cm) (for 6 in / 15 cm square origami paper).

**3**

To make the Head face the opposite direction, fold left and right in reverse from here.

Fold the paper edges to the center in steps ① and ②.

**4**

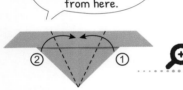

Fold the top flap along the dashed line.

**5**

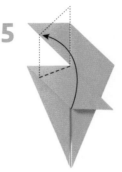

Fold back along the dashed line.

**6**

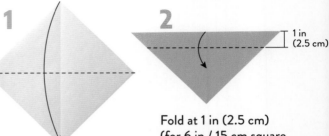

Fold along the dashed line.

**7**

Fold in small portions of the corners.

**8**

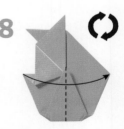

Fold in half and rotate the paper.

**9**

Fold small portions of the corners to the back.

**10**

The Head is completed. Draw on the face.

### Crossover ideas!

**Autumn Wreath made using another book**

Combine with other origami from different books for more fun!

**Owl (this book, page 38)**
Body:
6 × 6 in (15 × 15 cm)
Eyes and Beak Parts:
3 × 3 in (7.5 × 7.5 cm)

**From *Kamikey's Kawaii Seasonal Origami* (ISBN: 9784537218282):**
Leaf Wreath (page 99)
6 × 6 in (15 × 15 cm), 8 pieces

## Standing Body
Start from the Waterbomb Base (page 17).

**1**

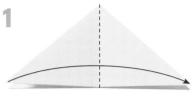

Fold the top left flap along the dashed line, like turning a page.

**2**

Fold the corner to the circled location.

**3**

Fold back the uppermost layer along the dashed line.

**4**

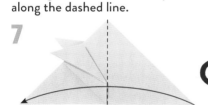

Leaving the bottommost flap, fold along the dashed line.

**5**

Fold the corner to the circled location.

**6**

Fold back the uppermost layer along the dashed line.

**7**

Fold in half, then rotate the paper.

**8**

The Standing Body is completed.

Cover the Body with the Clothes, glue it, and insert the Body into the pocket of the Head and glue it (the same goes for both standing and sitting versions).

## Sitting Body
Start from the completed Standing Body.

**1**

Fold along the dashed line. Do the same on the back.

**2**

The Sitting Body is completed. Turn it over.

_Finished!_

## Clothes
Start by folding in half vertically.

**1**

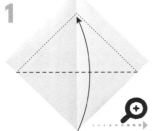

Fold along the dashed line.

**2**

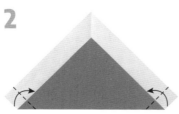

Fold along the dashed lines.

**3**

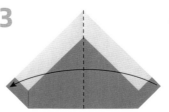

Fold in half.

**4**

The Clothes are completed.

## Mortar

Start by folding in half vertically and horizontally.

**1**

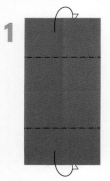

Fold behind to
the center.

**2**

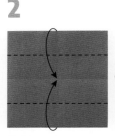

Fold to the center,
allowing the flaps
to swing out from
behind.

**3**

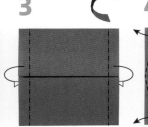

Fold backward along
the dashed lines, and
turn it over.

**4**

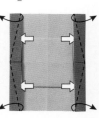

Open pockets from
the ⇦ ⇨ symbols and
flatten along the lines
between corners.

**5**

Turn it over.

## Pestle

**1**

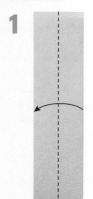

Fold in half.

**2**

Fold backward along
the dashed line.

**3**

Fold in half backward.

Finished!

## Cloud

Start from step **3** of the
Small Part of the Fan
(page 122).

**1**

Return the uppermost flaps.

**2**

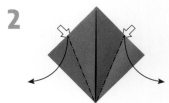

Open the pockets from the ⬃ ⬂
symbols and flatten.

**3**

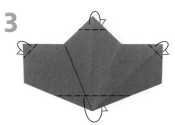

Fold backward along the dashed
lines.

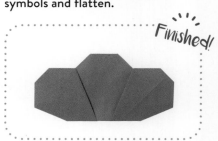

Finished!

Put it on the heads of various animals to make animal Santas!

Start by folding in half vertically.

**1**

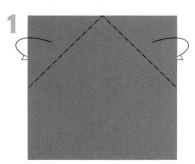

Fold the corners behind to the center.

**2**

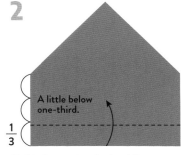

A little below one-third.

$\frac{1}{3}$

Fold along the dashed line.

**3**

②    $\frac{1}{3}$    ①

Fold backward at a one-third angle in steps ① and ②.

**4**

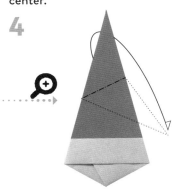

Fold backward along the dashed line.

**5**

Fold along the dashed line and insert the flap into the pocket.

Finished!

Put it on your favorite animals for Christmas decorations!

---

**Crossover ideas!**

**Christmas Wreath made using another book**

From *Kamikey's Heartfelt Gift Origami* (ISBN: 9784537219517):
**Holly Wreath (page 112)**
3 × 3 in (7.5 × 7.5 cm), 12 pieces

**Santa Hat**
3 × 3 in (7.5 × 7.5 cm)

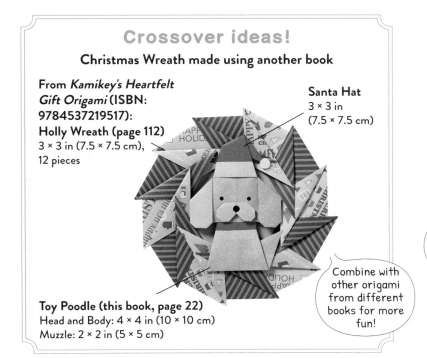

**Toy Poodle (this book, page 22)**
Head and Body: 4 × 4 in (10 × 10 cm)
Muzzle: 2 × 2 in (5 × 5 cm)

Combine with other origami from different books for more fun!

It also looks cute when glued to cards!

# Reindeer
Photo on page 131

We are essential parts of Christmas decorations!

## Head
Start from the Waterbomb Base (page 17).

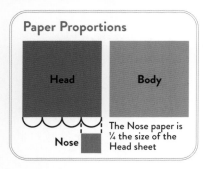

Paper Proportions

Head

Body

Nose

The Nose paper is ¼ the size of the Head sheet

**1**

Fold the edges of the top flaps to the center.

**2**

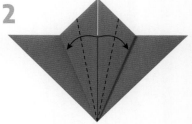

Bisect the angles.

**3**

Fold along the dashed line.

**4**

Fold along the dashed line so that the corners overlap.

**5**

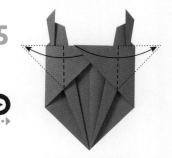

Fold back along the dashed lines.

**6**

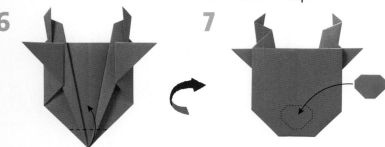

Fold the corner, and turn it over.

**7**

Attach the Nose.

**8**

The Head is completed. Draw on the face.

## Nose
Start from the Blintz Base (page 16).

**1**

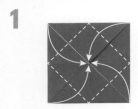

Fold the corners to the center.

**2**

Fold the top corner to the center, fold in small portions of the others, and turn it over.

**3**

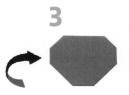

The Nose is completed.

Finished!

Attach the Head to the Body.

# Body

Start from step **5** of the Heart Rabbit (page 120).

Start from step **5** of the Heart Rabbit (page 120).

If you fold everything in reverse from the beginning, it will face right.

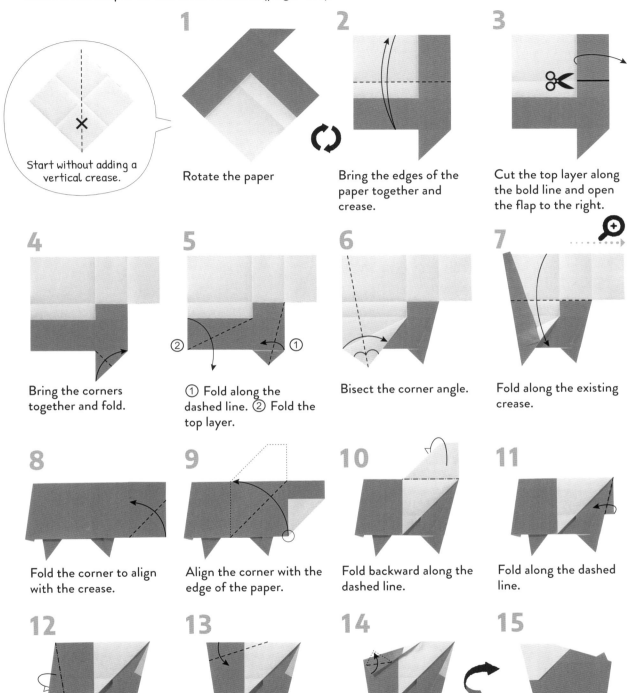

Start without adding a vertical crease.

**1** Rotate the paper

**2** Bring the edges of the paper together and crease.

**3** Cut the top layer along the bold line and open the flap to the right.

**4** Bring the corners together and fold.

**5** ① Fold along the dashed line. ② Fold the top layer.

**6** Bisect the corner angle.

**7** Fold along the existing crease.

**8** Fold the corner to align with the crease.

**9** Align the corner with the edge of the paper.

**10** Fold backward along the dashed line.

**11** Fold along the dashed line.

**12** Fold backward along the dashed line, and then tuck it into the underlying pocket.

**13** Fold along the dashed line.

**14** Fold back so that the corner sticks out, and turn it over.

**15** The Body is completed.

You can place animals on the sleigh or combine it with the reindeer for decoration.

## Part A

Start by folding in half horizontally.

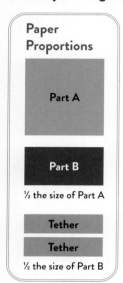

**Paper Proportions**

Part A

Part B

½ the size of Part A

Tether

Tether

½ the size of Part B

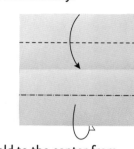

**1** Fold to the center from both the front and back.

**2** 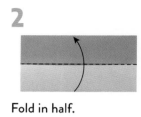 Fold in half.

**3**  Fold the top layer in half.

**4** 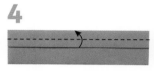 Fold the top flap in half.

**5** Fold only the bottom flap backward along the dashed lines.

**6** Part A is completed.

## Part B

Start by folding in half vertically and horizontally.

**1** 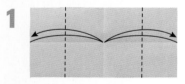 Fold to the center. Unfold.

**2** Fold to the center.

**3**  Align the side edges of the paper with the creases and fold.

**4**  Fold the overlapping corners to the outside edges.

**5**  Grasp the triangular flaps, pull them to the outside, and flatten.

**6**  Step **5** in progress.

**7**  Fold backward along the dashed line.

**8**  Part B is completed.

*Finished!*

Attach Part A to Part B.

☞ Continues

With just four parts, you can make a decent-sized wreath.

## Part A

Prepare two sheets of the same size paper.

The colors of Part A and Part B are different for clarity, but use your favorite colors and patterns.

**1**

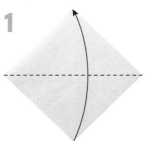

Fold in half.

**2**

Fold in half and make a pinch mark only at the dashed part.

**3**

Fold all layers of the top corner to the bottom edge.

**4**

Part A is completed. Make two of these.

## Part B

Prepare two sheets of the same size paper, starting from the completed Part A.

**1**

Bring the corners together and fold.

**2**

Part B is completed. Make two of these.

## Assembly

**1**

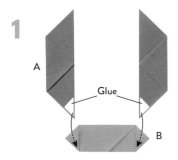

Glue

Position as shown in the photo, insert the corners of the Part A pieces into the pockets of Part B, and attach them with glue.

**2**

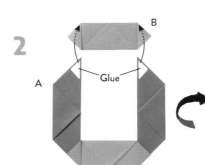

Glue

Insert the free corners of the Part A pieces into the pockets of another Part B piece, glue them together, and turn it over.

**Finished!**

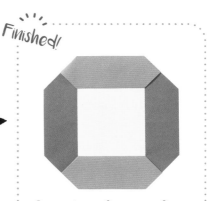

Cut a piece of paper to fit the back, and glue it in place.

When decorating with the reindeer:

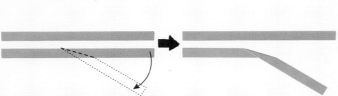

Make two A Parts of the Pole (page 129), fold one along the dashed line to make a set of Tethers.

Place animals on the sleigh!

Glue to the Reindeer (page 138) and the Sleigh using the Tethers.

141

Use it as a rectangular "wreath" or as a photo frame!

## Part A

Start by folding in half vertically and horizontally.

**1**

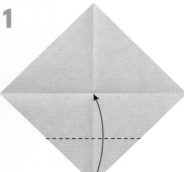

Fold the bottom corner to the center.

**2**

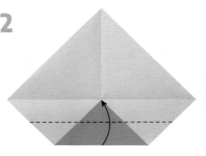

Fold the bottom edge of the paper to the horizontal crease.

**3**

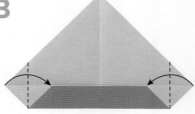

Fold along the dashed lines.

**4**

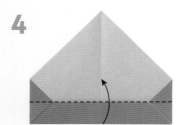

Fold along the existing crease.

**5**

Fold along the dashed line.

**6**

Fold the top corner to the edge of the flap.

**7**

Fold along the dashed line.

**8**

Flip it over.

**9**

Part A is completed. Make two of the same.

The instructions use different colored parts for clarity, but you should use your favorite colors or patterned paper and experiment with color combinations.

## Part B
Start after folding Part A through step **2**.

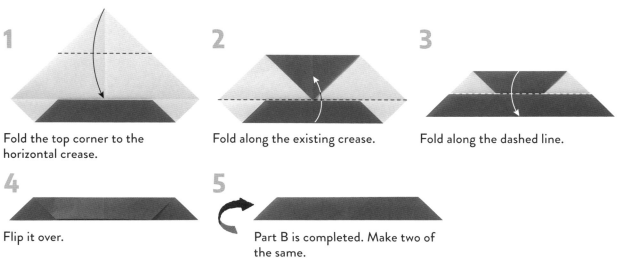

**1** Fold the top corner to the horizontal crease.

**2** Fold along the existing crease.

**3** Fold along the dashed line.

**4** Flip it over.

**5** Part B is completed. Make two of the same.

## Assembly Method

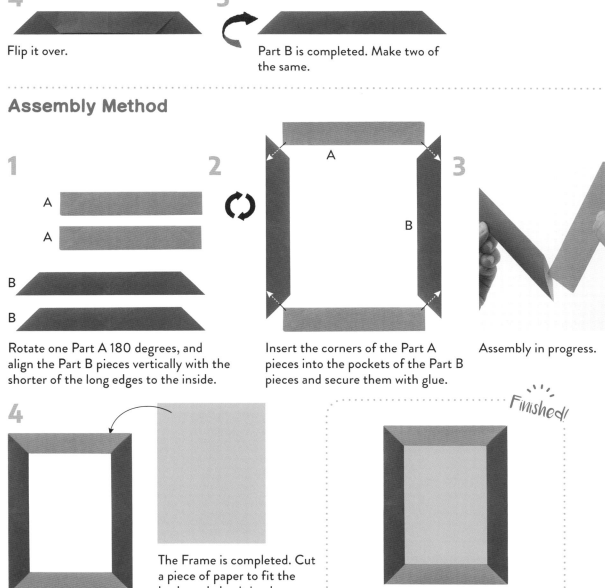

**1** Rotate one Part A 180 degrees, and align the Part B pieces vertically with the shorter of the long edges to the inside.

**2** Insert the corners of the Part A pieces into the pockets of the Part B pieces and secure them with glue.

**3** Assembly in progress.

**4** The Frame is completed. Cut a piece of paper to fit the back, and glue it in place.

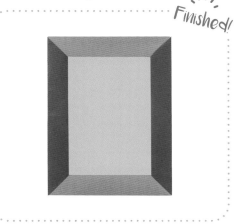

Finished!

## About the Author

Kamikey is an origami artist based in Sapporo who joined YouTube in 2015. Among her original origami models, about 450 have been turned into how-to videos. Initially active as a craft artist specializing in knitted items like amigurumi, she became engrossed in origami creation triggered by her embrace of motherhood. Leveraging her experience as a craft artist, she has created a unique world of origami decorations, and gained popularity with videos that are easy to understand even for beginners, including those having only previously folded the most basic models. Kamikey's cute artistic style and suggestions for combining decorations resonates with all sorts of folders, and women in particular. She continues to share her creative origami on social media platforms like Instagram and in magazines. Her books include *Kamikey's Seasonal Origami, Kamikey's Kawaii Seasonal Origami* and *Kamikey's Heartfelt Gift Origami* (all published in Japanese by Nihon Bungeisha).

### "Books to Span the East and West"

**Tuttle Publishing** was founded in 1832 in the small New England town of Rutland, Vermont [USA]. Our core values remain as strong today as they were then—to publish best-in-class books which bring people together one page at a time. In 1948, we established a publishing outpost in Japan—and Tuttle is now a leader in publishing English-language books about the arts, languages and cultures of Asia. The world has become a much smaller place today and Asia's economic and cultural influence has grown. Yet the need for meaningful dialogue and information about this diverse region has never been greater. Over the past seven decades, Tuttle has published thousands of books on subjects ranging from martial arts and paper crafts to language learning and literature—and our talented authors, illustrators, designers and photographers have won many prestigious award. We welcome you to explore the wealth of information available on Asia at **www.tuttlepublishing.com**.

Published by Tuttle Publishing, an imprint of Periplus Editions (HK) Ltd.

**www.tuttlepublishing.com**

978-4-8053-1906-2

Kamikey no Kawaii Tanoshii Dobutsu Origami
Copyright © 2023 Kamikey
English translation rights arranged with NIHONBUNGEISHA Co., Ltd., Tokyo through Japan UNI Agency, Inc., Tokyo

English translation © 2024 Periplus Editions (HK) Ltd

Printed in China    2412EP
28 27 26 25 24    10 9 8 7 6 5 4 3 2 1

TUTTLE PUBLISHING® is a registered trademark of Tuttle Publishing, a division of Periplus Editions (HK) Ltd.

**Distributed by**

**North America, Latin America & Europe**
Tuttle Publishing
364 Innovation Drive
North Clarendon,
VT 05759−9436 U.S.A.
Tel: (802) 773−8930
Fax: (802) 773−6993
info@tuttlepublishing.com
www.tuttlepublishing.com

**Japan**
Tuttle Publishing
Yaekari Building, 3rd Floor
5−4−12 Osaki
Shinagawa−ku
Tokyo 141−0032
Tel: (81) 3 5437−0171
Fax: (81) 3 5437−0755
sales@tuttle.co.jp
www.tuttle.co.jp

**Asia Pacific**
Berkeley Books Pte. Ltd.
3 Kallang Sector #04−01
Singapore 349278
Tel: (65) 6741−2178
Fax: (65) 6741−2179
inquiries@periplus.com.sg
www.tuttlepublishing.com